THE REDACTION OF GENESIS

THE REDACTION OF GENESIS

by

GARY A. RENDSBURG

EISENBRAUNS
Winona Lake, Indiana
1986

Library of Congress Cataloging-in-Publication Data

Rendsburg, Gary.
The redaction of Genesis.

Includes index.
1. Bible. O.T. Genesis—Criticism, Redaction. I. Title.
BS1235.2.R456 1986 222'.11066 86-9023
ISBN 0-931464-25-0

Dedicated to Cyrus H. Gordon

TABLE OF CONTENTS

ABBREVIATIONS ix
PREFACE xi
INTRODUCTION 1
CHAPTER I: THE PRIMEVAL HISTORY 7
CHAPTER II: THE ABRAHAM CYCLE 27
CHAPTER III: THE JACOB CYCLE 53
CHAPTER IV: THE LINKING MATERIAL 71
CHAPTER V: THE JOSEPH STORY 79
CHAPTER VI: REDACTIONAL STRUCTURING
AND SOURCE CRITICISM 99
CHAPTER VII: THE DATE OF GENESIS 107
INDEX 121

ABBREVIATIONS

BDB	F. Brown, S. R. Driver, and C. A. Briggs, *A Hebrew and English Lexicon of the Old Testament* (Oxford, 1906)
BHS	*Biblia Hebraica Stuttgartensia* (Stuttgart, 1977)
CBQ	*Catholic Biblical Quarterly*
EJ	*Encyclopaedia Judaica*
IEJ	*Israel Exploration Journal*
JANESCU	*Journal of the Ancient Near Eastern Society of Columbia University*
JBL	*Journal of Biblical Literature*
JJS	*Journal of Jewish Studies*
JNES	*Journal of Near Eastern Studies*
JQR	*Jewish Quarterly Review*
JSOT	*Journal for the Study of the Old Testament*
LB	*Linguistica Biblica*
NAB	*New American Bible* (New York, 1970)
NJPSV	*The Torah* (Philadelphia, 1962) = New Jewish Publication Society Version
OMRO	*Oudheidkundige Mededeelingen uit het Rijksmuseum van Oudheden te Leiden*
OTS	*Oudtestamentische Studien*
SAK	*Studien zur altägyptischen Kultur*
VT	*Vetus Testamentum*
VTSup	*Vetus Testamentum, Supplements*
ZAW	*Zeitschrift für die alttestamentliche Wissenschaft*

PREFACE

The present volume is a slender one, and not wholly original. It borrows greatly, as much of scholarship does, from previous work in the same field. In the case of the subject at hand, work by Umberto Cassuto, Nahum M. Sarna, Michael Fishbane, and Jack M. Sasson have paved the way for my own research. Not only am I greatly indebted to these individuals' writings, but I take this opportunity to thank Professors Sarna, Fishbane, and Sasson for their communications on the subject and for their encouragement.

The knowledgeable reader will realize that four of us who have contributed to this area of research are all students of the same man, Cyrus H. Gordon, and that the fifth was a close associate in the fields of Ugaritic and Biblical studies. Accordingly, it is a fitting tribute to dedicate this book to Professor Gordon. Furthermore, I have been aided by Dr. Gordon in various ways in recent years, and for this I am particularly grateful.

M. O'Connor read the manuscript of this book and made many insightful comments. His astute observations caused me to rethink several points, and those which have been incorporated have improved my work greatly. For the time and effort he put into this task, I am most thankful.

My typist, Lynne Glair, who knows no Hebrew and for whom Hebrew transliteration is most peculiar, produced an outstanding manuscript. This difficult task, encumbered by an abnormally large percentage of Hebrew words, was carried out most efficiently and always cheerfully. Her successor, Veronica Caldwell, was of assistance in the final stages of the book's preparation.

My friend, Dr. Gerald Berkowitz, performed the yeoman task of reading the volume in galley-proof; to him I offer my sincere thanks.

I am also indebted to two individuals at Canisius College, Rev. Benjamin Fiore, S.J., chairman of the Department of Religious Studies, and Dr. Walter G. Sharrow, dean of the College of Arts and Sciences, for decreasing my teaching load during the Fall 1982 semester and thus enabling me to write the better part of this volume. Fr. Fiore receives additional thanks for his assistance in the preparation of the Egyptian hieroglyphs adorning the dedication page.

Finally, as always, I express my love to Susan, whose love, devotion, and sacrifice know no bounds and are never ceasing.

INTRODUCTION

No book has attracted the attention of modern biblical scholarship more than Genesis. Its myths and legends, stories and genealogies, prose and poetry, have been fertile ground for many approaches: comparative, historical, archaeological, text-critical, source-critical, etc. But with the exception of the general conclusion that Genesis may be divided into four great cycles devoted to Primeval History, Abraham, Jacob, and Joseph,[1] literary criticism has been less productive. There have been occasional voices raised to show how attention to literary details reveals the artistry of the authors, but the literary approach to the Bible in general and to Genesis in particular has not been popular.

In recent years, the trend has shifted, and literary criticism is now recognized as its own discipline within the greater purview of biblical studies. Much of this work has been directed at Genesis, which is the biblical book best represented in such works as Robert Alter's *The Art of Biblical Narrative*, Michael Fishbane's *Text and Texture*, and the two volumes edited by K. R. R. Gros Louis entitled *Literary Interpretations of Biblical Narratives*, and is the sole

[1] See, e.g., E. A. Speiser, *Genesis* (Garden City, NY, 1964) liii–lx. G. W. Coats (*Genesis* [Grand Rapids, MI, 1983] 14, 16, 28–29, etc.) prefers to call the third cycle after Isaac (in accordance with Genesis' own wording at 25:19) and the fourth cycle after Jacob (see 37:2). Coats's book appeared after the bulk of the present volume was written; accordingly I have been unable to incorporate its ideas into my research.

subject of J. P. Fokkelman's *Narrative Art in Genesis.*[2] The present volume builds on the groundbreaking work effected by these authors, and hopes to further their efforts in demonstrating the gain which literary analysis of the Bible can yield.

My research is even more closely tied to several studies which deserve special mention here. Above, I noted that among the basic assumptions of Genesis scholarship is the book's division into four cycles. This has long been recognized, but recent literary analysis has gone one step further. Not only can the work of a compiler be seen in the book as a whole, but within a particular cycle there may also be considerable editorial arrangement.

In 1975 Michael Fishbane published his work on the Jacob Cycle (25:19–35:22),[3] in which he showed that the various stories concerning the third patriarch are all duplicates of one another, aligned in a chiastic order. That is to say, the first and last episodes share the same motifs and concerns, as do the second and next-to-last episodes, etc. Moreover, the relationship between these matching units is highlighted by a series of shared vocabulary items, or theme-words.

In 1980 Jack M. Sasson wrote a similar work on the Primeval History (1:1–11:9).[4] Here, too, there are matching units, again sharing related themes and various theme-words. In this instance, however, the individual units are not in chiastic structure, rather in parallel columns. Thus, the first and sixth episodes are paired, the second and seventh, the third and eighth, the fourth and ninth, the

[2] The full bibliographic particulars of these volumes appear in the footnotes in the chapters which follow.

[3] M. Fishbane, "Composition and Structure in the Jacob Cycle (Gen. 25:19–35:22)," *JJS* 26 (1975) 15–38, reprinted with some changes in M. Fishbane, *Text and Texture* (New York, 1979) 40–62.

[4] J. M. Sasson, "The 'Tower of Babel' as a Clue to the Redactional Structuring of the Primeval History (Gen. 1–11:9)," in *The Bible World: Essays in Honor of Cyrus H. Gordon* (ed. G. Rendsburg; New York, 1980) 211–19.

fifth and tenth. Sasson referred to the literary schema used by the compiler as "redactional structuring," a term which is gratefully borrowed throughout the present work.

The groundwork for redactional structuring in a third portion of Genesis had actually been laid years earlier by Umberto Cassuto.[5] This savant noted that the Abraham Cycle (12:1–22:19) also consisted of a series of episodes which, to a great extent, duplicate and parallel each other, again in chiastic order. Cassuto did not live to complete his work on Genesis, so there is no way to determine if he also would have noted theme-words linking the paired units. Nahum M. Sarna, in his highly praised commentary on Genesis,[6] had noticed, apparently independently of Cassuto, some of the same structure. He did point out shared vocabulary items, at least for 12:1–9 and 22:1–19.

In the pages that follow, I accept the basic conclusions of these scholars. Occasionally I have made adjustments to their work and always I have greatly expanded their ideas and multiplied their examples. Chapter I builds on Sasson's foundation to discuss the Primeval History, here including all of 1:1–11:26. Chapter II utilizes Cassuto's and Sarna's material to discuss the Abraham Cycle, here expanded to 11:27–22:24. Chapter III expands on Fishbane's treatment of the Jacob Cycle, 25:19–35:22.

Once it was determined that the first three cycles reveal a purposeful literary structure, the search for such a pattern in the one remaining cycle became an obvious task. The results of this work are incorporated into Chapter V, where I have illustrated how the units of the Joseph Story, 37:1–50:26, are also paired, aligned chiastically, with interrelated theme-words. The remaining parts of Genesis, what I call the Linking Material of 23:1–25:18

[5] U. Cassuto, *From Noah to Abraham* (Jerusalem, 1964) 296.
[6] N. M. Sarna, *Understanding Genesis* (New York, 1966) 160–61.

and 35:23–36:43, are discussed in Chapter IV. Even here the compiler has worked matching units into his schema. The result is the realization that all of Genesis is brilliantly constructed, the accomplishment of an ancient Israelite genius who formed the book into a literary whole.

The presentation of this material is the same for each of the first five chapters. Let us assume a paradigm cycle of ten episodes or units, which are aligned in the order ABCDEE′D′C′B′A′. (The order of the Primeval History, the only one without chiasm, would be ABCDEA′B′-C′D′E′.) Each chapter begins with such an outline, presenting the matched units. I then proceed to the meatiest part of each chapter, the presentation of each pair of matched units within each cycle, first A and A′, then B and B′, etc. After a brief discussion of the parallel ideas, motifs, and story lines, I present the theme-words which highlight the relationship between the two units. First I list those theme-words which have been adduced by previous scholars (mainly Sasson for Primeval History, Sarna for Abraham Cycle, and Fishbane for Jacob Cycle), and then I advance my own contributions. This division of the material tends to fracture the discussion somewhat, but I felt it important to emphasize the work of previous scholars. My listing of the theme-words also makes the discussion less prosaic, but the utilization of lists was the most efficient way to organize the enormous amount of material which developed. Furthermore, I have chosen not to weigh the individual theme-words and thus they are not ranked in order of importance. Instead, they are listed in verse order, i.e., in the order in which they occur in the text, specifically in the first of the matched units under discussion. My sense is that, with few exceptions, the authors of these stories intended the various theme-words to operate collectively. They connect the matched units as a group, not just as single words.

Once the redactional structuring by matched units has been demonstrated, I next point out the midway point, coming between E and E′, upon which the entire cycle pivots. In each instance, as would be expected, this focus comes at a crucial place in the developing story.

Finally, there is another series of vocabulary items featured in redactional structuring. Not only do theme-words link units A and A′, B and B′, etc., but other words, called catchwords, link successive units, i.e., A and B, B and C, etc., through D′ and E′. These entries are also noted, for they act as bridges which aid the linear flow of the cycle from unit to unit.

Since so much of redactional structuring is tied to theme-words and catchwords, a description of these items is appropriate. They can be of several types. The most obvious are those where the same word is used in matching or successive episodes. Others are different words or, to use more precise grammatical terminology, different inflections, from the same root. Some theme-words and catchwords can be like-sounding words which derive from separate roots, and still others may be merely similar in meaning or share a similar connotation. What links all of these variations is the ability to connect, if the writer or compiler has achieved his goal, the different units of the cycle.

While one of the aims of this book is to demonstrate the redactional structure of Genesis, we would be lessening its importance if we did not discuss the implications of this discovery. Accordingly, in each chapter I occasionally point out critical problems which disappear in light of the literary analysis undertaken. But the most important implication of redactional structuring is its bearing on source criticism. This latter endeavor has tended to view the text through a microscope, breaking it apart into tiny pieces, which are then assigned customarily to J, E, or P. The literary approach pulls back the lens, and the wide-angle view results in a greater appreciation of how the literary creation works as a whole. These contrasting approaches and the reasons why literary criticism renders the usual approach to source criticism untenable, are the subject of Chapter VI. Finally, an additional section, Chapter VII, on the date of Genesis' redaction, is included.

Having laid out the background of this endeavor and the principle methods by which the material is presented, let us progress to individual discussions of each of the cycles. For it is in these chapters that the methodology and the results thereof will become self-apparent.[7]

[7] Two important volumes have not been utilized in this study, but should be mentioned here. J. W. Welch, ed., *Chiasmus in Antiquity* (Hildesheim, 1981), came to my attention after this book was written; especially germane is the article by Y. T. Radday, "Chiasmus in Hebrew Biblical Narrative," pp. 50–117. I. M. Kikawada and A. Quinn, *Before Abraham Was* (Nashville, 1985), appeared when the present volume was in press; it too argues for the essential unity of Genesis 1–11.

I

THE PRIMEVAL HISTORY

Scholars have long recognized that the first eleven chapters of Genesis form an integrated unit. Whereas from Genesis 12 on the Bible is concerned solely with the nation of Israel, the opening of Scripture deals with topics of a more universalistic nature. The creation of the world, and the flood which destroyed it and gave it a new start, affected everyone, not just Israel. God's covenant with Israel, which dominates the Bible, receives no mention until Genesis 15 and is not even hinted at until Genesis 12. What occurs in Genesis 1–11, instead, is God's covenant with all of humanity. Even in the Table of Nations in Genesis 10, where all the peoples of the world are enumerated, Israel is conspicuously absent. These and other factors have led scholars to set these chapters apart from the remainder of Genesis, the Pentateuch, and indeed the entire Hebrew Bible.[1]

But as widely recognized as the independence and cohesiveness of the Primeval History has been, it took until 1980 for someone to point out that the arrangement of these stories reveals a deliberate literary structure. It was Jack Sasson who first noticed that "the episodes culled from Hebraic traditions of early history were conceived

[1] J. Morgenstern, *The Book of Genesis* (New York, 1965) 21–24; E. A. Speiser, *Genesis* (Garden City, NY, 1964) liii–lviii; R. Davidson, *Genesis 1–11* (Cambridge, 1973) 8–9; D. Kidner, *Genesis* (Downers Grove, IL, 1967) 13; and M. Fishbane, *Text and Texture* (New York, 1979) 17–39.

in two matching sequences."[2] I accept Sasson's basic premise—for it is undeniable—but in what follows I alter some of the details and greatly expand on the material which can be presented to show the mastery of our redactor's hand.

Gen 1:1–11:26 consists of ten smaller units, each with its own parallel, which accordingly can be aligned into five episodes which are then repeated. The redactor of the Primeval History has structured these units in the following manner:

A Creation, God's Words to Adam (1:1–3:24)
B Adam's Sons (4:1–16)
C Technological Development of Mankind (4:17–26)
D Ten Generations from Adam to Noah (5:1–32)
E Downfall: The Nephilim (6:1–8)
A′ Flood, God's Words to Noah (6:9–9:17)
B′ Noah's Sons (9:18–29)
C′ Ethnic Development of Mankind (10:1–32)
E′ Downfall: Tower of Babel (11:1–9)
D′ Ten Generations from Noah to Terah (11:10–26)

Gen 1:1–6:8 gives us five units which are then duplicated in 6:9–11:26. Moreover, with one exception, this repetition occurs in the same order. The exception (D′) is necessarily out of sequence and will be discussed below. The stories are duplicated not only regarding theme and general story line, but key vocabulary items or theme-words in the individual units are repeated to highlight the method of compilation. Let us move to discussions of each of the matching episodes where the redactional structuring is readily seen.

[2] J. M. Sasson, "The 'Tower of Babel' as a Clue to the Redactional Structuring of the Primeval History (Gen. 1–11:9)," in *The Bible World: Essays in Honor of Cyrus H. Gordon* (ed. G. Rendsburg; New York, 1980) 211–19, especially 218. A similar pattern is detected by R. L. Cohn, "Narrative Structure and Canonical Perspective in Genesis," *JSOT* 25 (1983) 5.

A CREATION, GOD'S WORDS TO ADAM (1:1–3:24)

A′ FLOOD, GOD'S WORDS TO NOAH (6:9–9:17)

To point out that these two episodes parallel each other is nothing new. Commentators on Genesis have demonstrated the relationships between them many times. The Flood is a second Creation, a new beginning; and Noah is a second Adam. Parallel thoughts and theme-words which previous scholars have adduced are as follows:

i. *rûaḥ ʾĕlōhîm*, 'wind of God,' occurs in 1:2; and *rûaḥ*, 'wind,' occurs in 8:1, where the word immediately preceding it is *ʾĕlōhîm*, 'God.'[3]

ii. *tᵉhôm*, 'Tehom (abyss),' appears in 1:2; and the same word appears in 7:11, 8:2.[4]

iii. In 1:9 God gathers the waters to one place and the dry land becomes visible; in 8:13 the waters recede and the dry land again becomes visible.[5]

iv. God says *pᵉrû ûrᵉbû*, 'be fruitful and multiply,' to the animals in 1:22; in 8:17 speaking about the animals, God says *ûpārû wᵉrābû*, 'let them be fruitful and multiply.'[6]

v. God says *pᵉrû ûrᵉbû ûmilʾû ʾet hâʾāreṣ*, 'be fruitful and multiply, and fill the earth,' to the humans in 1:28; and the same words are spoken to Noah and his sons in 9:1.[7]

vi. The humans are given mastery over the animals in

[3] U. Cassuto, *From Noah to Abraham* (Jerusalem, 1964) 101; Fishbane, *Text and Texture*, 33; and Sasson, "Redactional Structuring," 216.

[4] Davidson, *Genesis 1–11*, 80; Fishbane, *Text and Texture*, 33; Sasson, "Redactional Structuring," 216; and Morgenstern, *Genesis*, 82.

[5] Sasson, "Redactional Structuring," 216.

[6] Davidson, *Genesis 1–11*, 84; Kidner, *Genesis*, 92; and Sasson, "Redactional Structuring," 216.

[7] Cassuto, *From Noah to Abraham*, 124; Kidner, *Genesis*, 100; Fishbane, *Text and Texture*, 34; and Sasson, "Redactional Structuring," 216.

1:28; and Noah and his sons receive the same in 9:2.[8]

vii. The root *šbt*, 'rest, cease,' appears at the end of (at least one) Creation in 2:2–3; and the same root occurs at the end of the Flood in 8:22.[9]

But there are many other parallels in A and A′ which can be cited.

viii. *kol nepeš haḥayyâ hârômeśet . . . lᵉmînēhem*, 'every living thing which creeps . . . according to its kind,' are created on the fifth day in 1:21; and *kol remeś hâʾădāmâ lᵉmînēhû*, 'every creeper of the earth according to its kind,' are brought on board the ark in 6:20 (cf. 7:14).

ix. *kol ʿôp kānāp lᵉmînēhû*, 'every winged fowl according to its kind,' are created also on the fifth day in 1:21; and *hāʿôp lᵉmînēhû*, 'the fowl according to its kind,' are brought on board the ark in 6:20, 7:14.

x. *ḥayyat hâʾāreṣ lᵉmînāh*, 'the beasts of the earth each according to its kind,' are created on the sixth day in 1:25; and *kol haḥayyah lᵉmînāh*, 'every beast according to its kind,' board the ark in 7:14.

xi. The last group of animals is *habbᵉhēmâ lᵉmînāh*, 'the cattle according to its kind,' which are created on the sixth day in 1:25; and which board the ark in 6:20, 7:14.

xii. Near the end of the first Creation account we have the statement *bᵉṣelem ʾĕlōhîm bārāʾ ʾôtô*, 'in the image of God he created him,' in 1:27; and toward the end of the Flood story we read *bᵉṣelem ʾĕlōhîm ʿāśâ ʾet hâʾādām*, 'in the image of God he made man,' in 9:6.

xiii. The expression *zākār ûnᵉqēbâ*, 'male and female,' occurs in 1:27; and then four times in the Flood account in 6:19, 7:3, 7:9, 7:16.

xiv. After Creation is completed we read *wayᵉbārek ʾōtām ʾĕlôhîm wayyōʾmer lāhem*, 'God blessed them and said to them,' in 1:28; and after the Flood we read *wayᵉbārek ʾĕlōhîm ʾet nōaḥ wᵉʾet bānāw wayyōʾmer lāhem*, 'God blessed Noah and his sons and said to them,' in 9:1.

[8] Cassuto, *From Noah to Abraham*, 126; Davidson, *Genesis 1–11*, 88–89; Fishbane, *Text and Texture*, 34; and Sasson, "Redactional Structuring," 217.

[9] Cassuto, *From Noah to Abraham*, 123; and Sasson, "Redactional Structuring," 217.

xv. The words spoken after 1:28 and 9:1 include a description of which foods may be eaten and the phrase *yîhᵉyeh lᵉʾoklâ*, 'shall be for food,' occurs in both 1:29 and 9:3.

xvi. The roots *ʿśh* and *klh*, 'make' and 'complete,' are collocated in 2:1–2 and also in 6:16.

xvii. *yôm haššᵉbîʿî*, 'the seventh day,' climaxes Creation in 2:2–3; and *šibʿat (hay)yāmîm*, '(the) seven days,' occurs throughout the Flood story in 7:10, 8:10, 8:12.

xviii. At the beginning of the second Creation story we have the third-person statement *lôʾ himṭîr YHWH ʾĕlōhîm ʿal hâʾāreṣ*, 'Yahweh Elohim had not brought rain upon the earth,' in 2:5; near the beginning of the Flood story we have a similar statement couched in first-person terms *ʾānōkî mamṭîr ʿal hâʾāreṣ*, 'I will bring rain upon the earth,' in 7:4.

xix. *bᵉʾappāw nišmat ḥayyîm*, 'in his nostrils the breath of life,' occurs in 2:7; and *nišmat rûaḥ ḥayyîm bᵉʾappāw*, 'the breath of the spirit of life in its nostrils,' occurs in 7:22.

xx. The verbal root *yṣr*, 'create,' obtains in 2:7–8; and the noun *yēṣer* occurs in 8:21.

xxi. The verb *wayyisgōr*, 'he closed,' is predicated of Yahweh Elohim in 2:21 (closing the man's flesh); the same verb is used in 7:16 (closing the ark) where it is immediately preceded by Elohim and immediately followed by Yahweh.

xxii. Albeit with different connotations the word *ʿeṣem* occurs in 2:23 (meaning 'bone') and in 7:13 (meaning 'same').

xxiii. Two words after *ʿeṣem* in 2:23 comes *bāśār*, 'flesh'; and soon after *ʿeṣem* in the Flood account comes *bāśār*, 'flesh,' in 7:15–16.

xxiv. The important word *mithallēk*, 'moving,' occurs in 3:8; and in 6:9 we have *hithallek*, 'moving, walking.'

xxv. At the very end of the Creation stories there appears the *ḥereb*, 'sword,' an instrument of war, in 3:24; and the Flood epic closes with the placement of the *qešet*, 'bow,' another instrument of war, in 9:13–16.[10]

[10] See G. von Rad, *Genesis* (Philadelphia, 1961) 130; Fishbane, *Text and Texture*, 34; and Davidson, *Genesis 1–11*, 92; though none of these authors makes the connection with the sword in 3:24.

xxvi. *derek*, 'way,' occurs in 3:24; and *darkô*, 'his way,' appears in 6:12.

These 26 times demonstrate conclusively the close correlations between 1:1–3:24 (A) and 6:9–9:17 (A'). Similar themes occur in both stories. A tells of the watery mass which emerges as earth, of the creation of the animals and of man, and of God's instructions to man. A' also depicts a watery mass which emerges as earth; it tells of the salvation of those very same animals, and it repeats the same or similar instructions to man. Theme-words serve to link the two accounts, sometimes with the same connotation such as *rûaḥ*, *tᵉhôm*, *ṣelem ᵓelōhîm*, *himṭîr/mamṭîr*, etc., and sometimes with slightly different or even very different connotations as with the roots *šbt*, *yṣr*, *ᶜśh*, *klh*, and the words *ᶜeṣem* and *mithallēk/hithallek*.

By recognizing the intimate relationship between A and A' we are also able to solve a redactional problem which has plagued biblical scholars for more than a century now. 1:1–3:24 is readily divisible into two different stories, 1:1–2:4a and 2:4b–3:24. 6:9–9:17 is not as easily divided, but as E. A. Speiser has written, "The received biblical account of the Flood is beyond reasonable doubt a composite narrative, reflecting more than one separate source." He goes on to state that whereas the two Creation myths are merely connected one to another, with the Flood "the two strands have become intertwined, the end result being a skillful and intricate patchwork."[11] Evidence for the two sources are the following duplications and repetitions: 1) 6:19–21 and 7:1–3 both tell of the food and animals which are to be brought aboard the ark; 2) 6:22 and 7:5 both state that Noah did everything he was commanded; 3) 6:17–18 and 7:4 both give us God's warning that he will destroy the earth; 4) 7:6–12 and 7:13–24 both describe the entrance into the ark and the coming of the flood; and 5) 8:1–12 and 8:13–14 both tell of the waters receding, Noah's opening up the ark, and the drying of the earth.

[11] Speiser, *Genesis*, 54.

Scholars have asked why two Creation stories were necessary and the answer seems to be that our compiler wished to include one theocentric account (1:1–2:4a) and one anthropocentric account (2:4b–3:24). This is even implied by the introductions to the two myths, the first referring to "heaven and earth" in 1:1 and 2:4a and the second to "earth and heaven" in 2:4b.[12]

But what would be the rationale for including duplications and repetitions in the Flood story? Given the redactional structuring of Genesis 1–11 and more specifically the analogy of 1:1–3:24 and 6:9–9:17, our compiler needed two Flood stories because he had two Creation stories. But he could not simply connect the two Flood stories as he had done with the two Creation stories. The latter, even with their differences, were not seen as mutually exclusive by the Hebrews and could thus be placed side-by-side. But to have done the same with the two Flood stories would have confused matters too much, for it would have required two fresh starts, two covenants, perhaps even two Noahs, etc., and so the solution was to intertwine the two accounts into one Flood story.[13]

The relationship between A and A′ is further cemented. In short, there are three areas which unite the Creation and Flood myths within the Primeval History: the overall theme of the start of the world, key vocabulary items, and duplicates.

B ADAM'S SONS (4:1–16)
B′ NOAH'S SONS (9:18–29)

As discussed in the preceding section, the Flood is a repeat of Creation and Noah is depicted as a second Adam. The units which respectively follow the Creation

[12] Speiser, *Genesis*, 18–19.

[13] That the Flood story itself reflects redactional structuring has been demonstrated by G. J. Wenham, "The Coherence of the Flood Narrative," *VT* 28 (1978) 336–48. I thank Professor C. Hassell Bullock

and Flood epics are also parallel, each dealing with the sons of the protagonist. In each story there is discord between brothers, one leading to fratricide, one leading to enslavement.[14] Theme-words again serve to highlight the relationship between the two episodes.

i. The sons of Adam are introduced at the beginning of the story in 4:1–2; and the sons of Noah are named at the beginning of the second story in 9:18.

ii. *ʾădāmâ*, 'soil,' and specifically the tilling of the soil occurs in 4:3 and 9:20.

iii. *minḥâ*, 'offering,' in 4:3 and *minḥātô*, 'his offering,' in 4:4–5, are important since they serve the author as the agent which led to the brotherly strife; from a different root but serving the same purpose is *nôaḥ*, 'Noah,' in 9:18–29. A number of other words denoting sacrifice could have been used in 4:3–5, such as *zebaḥ*, 'sacrifice,' or *ʿōlâ*, 'holocaust,' but *minḥâ* is utilized in assonance with *nôaḥ*.

iv. *petaḥ*, 'opening,' in 4:7 suggests perhaps a tent opening; in 9:21 we have the desired *ʾohŏlōh*, 'his tent.' The expression *petaḥ (hā)ʾôhel*, 'opening of the tent,' is common in the Pentateuch and perhaps the division of this phrase in B and B′ is by design.

v. In 4:8 we read *wayyōʾmer qayin ʾel hebel ʾāḥîw*, 'Cain said to his brother Abel'; in 9:22 we read *wayyaggēd lišnê ʾeḥāw*, 'he told his two brothers.'

vi. Central to B is the red liquid, blood, in 4:10; and central to B′ is the red liquid, wine, in 9:24.

vii. *ʾārûr*, 'cursed,' occurs in both 4:11 and 9:25.

viii. In 4:11 we have *min hâʾădāmâ ʾăšer pāṣᵉtâ*, 'from the land which opened'; and in 9:19 we have *nāpᵉṣâ kol hâʾāreṣ*, 'the whole earth branched out.' The words *pāṣᵉtâ* and *nāpᵉṣâ* come from different roots, *pṣh* and *npṣ* respectively, but are in assonance and have as their subjects either "land" or "earth."

ix. The root *ʿbd*, 'work, serve,' occurs in 4:12 and 9:25; in each case it is the punishment for the committed crime.

---

of Wheaton College for pointing this reference out to me. For a weaker attempt at finding literary patterns in this material, see N. W. Lund, *Chiasmus in the New Testament* (Chapel Hill, NC, 1942) 60–62.

[14] Sasson, "Redactional Structuring," 215–16, 217.

x. The hiding or turning of one's face occurs in 4:14 and 9:23.

A recognition of the interconnections between A and A′ helped solve a major problem in the Flood epic. Similarly we may utilize the rapport between B and B′ to help solve a problem in the Cain and Abel story. Textual critics have been plagued by 4:8 where the text reads "Cain said to his brother Abel," but no words follow. Solutions range from invoking the versions which all supply the missing words,[15] to emending *wayyōʾmer* to another verb,[16] to translating *wayyōʾmer* not as 'said' but rather 'saw' based on the Akkadian cognate.[17]

But if we compare 4:8 to 9:22 as is done above, we may solve this crux. In the latter verse we read "he (Ham) told his brothers," but here too we are not informed what was said. Admittedly we do not need a direct quote following the verb *wayyaggēd*, 'he told,' but it is still not clear what Ham told Shem and Japheth. Did he tell them that Noah was drunk? that Noah was naked? that he saw Noah naked? What was the tone of his voice? We are informed of none of these things, but we can infer what was said and how it was said from the succeeding verses. The same holds in 4:8. Our author does not want to apprise us of what was said, but from what follows we can surmise it was not a friendly chat. In other words, the missing words in 4:8 are deliberately missing.

C TECHNOLOGICAL DEVELOPMENT OF MANKIND (4:17–26)

C′ ETHNIC DEVELOPMENT OF MANKIND (10:1–32)

The episode of Adam's sons is followed by a discussion of mankind's development along technological

[15] Speiser, *Genesis*, 30–31.

[16] H. Gunkel, *Genesis* (Göttingen, 1910) 44.

[17] M. Dahood, "Abraham's Reply in Genesis 20,11," *Biblica* 61 (1980) 90. Cassuto (*From Adam to Noah*, 215) cites the same cognate but strains to translate *wayyōʾmer* as 'appointed a place where to meet.'

grounds. The episode of Noah's sons is followed by a discussion of mankind's development along ethnic grounds. Apart from the very general comparison, at first glance there does not seem to be much material to link C and C′. But a deeper investigation turns up some very interesting parallels.

There is really only one story line included in C′, the Table of Nations, namely that concerning Nimrod in 10:8–12; the rest of the material is comprised of lists. But in this one story of a few verses we have a number of vocabulary items which are shared by 4:17–26.

i. *hēḥēl*, 'he began,' occurs in 10:8; and *hûḥal*, 'began,' appears in 4:26.
ii. Nimrod was a hero *lipnê YHWH*, 'before Yahweh,' in 10:9; and Cain goes out *millipnê YHWH*, 'from before Yahweh,' in 4:16.
iii. Nimrod resides *bᵉʾereṣ šinʿār*, 'in the land of Shinar,' in 10:10; and Cain dwells *bᵉʾereṣ nôd qidmat ʿēden*, 'in the land of Nod east of Eden,' in 4:16. We cannot pinpoint the location of Nod east of Eden, but it is certainly in Mesopotamia (see 2:10–14) which is intended by biblical Shinar (= Sumer) (see 11:1–9).
iv. *yāṣāʾ*, 'he went out,' is predicated of Nimrod in 10:11; and *wayyēṣēʾ*, 'he went out,' is predicated of Cain in 4:16.
v. In 10:11 Nimrod builds (*wayyiben*) the cities of Nineveh, Rehoboth-ir, Calah, and Resen; in 4:17 Cain builds (*wayᵉhî bôneh*) the city of Enoch.

There is one other verse in 10:1–32 which does not fully belong to the catalogued material and that is 10:21, *ûlᵉšēm yullad gam hûʾ ʾăbî kol bᵉnê ʿēber ʾăḥî yepet haggādôl*, 'and to Shem, also to him were born, the father of all the children of Eber, the older brother of Japheth.' This verse introduces Shem but it is unlike 10:2 which begins simply *bᵉnê yepet*, 'the sons of Japheth,' or 10:6 which begins *ûbᵉnê ḥām*, 'and the sons of Ham,' U. Cassuto comments on the special character of this verse.

Because of the exceptional importance of Shem, the Bible was not content with a simple phrase, like 'And the sons of Shem', for the preamble to the paragraph, in the style of the formula found above, *The sons of Japheth, And the sons of Ham.* Instead, the roll of the sons of Shem is prefaced by this complete verse, which serves as a formal introduction, mentioning together with Shem's name all his other designations.[18]

But we may go even further. Just as the Nimrod notice sticks out within the Table of Nations and thus has shared theme-words in 4:16–26, so does 10:21 share theme-words with C. We may continue our list.

vi. 10:21 begins *ûlᵉšēm yullad gam hûʾ*, 'and to Shem, also to him were born'; and in 4:26 we read *ûlᵉšēt gam hûʾ yullad bēn*, 'and to Seth, also to him was born a son.'

vii. In 10:21 Shem is described as *ʾăbî kol bᵉnê ʿēber*, 'the father of all the children of Eber'; and in 4:22 we read that Jubal was *ʾăbî kol tôpēś kinnôr wᵉʿûgāb*, 'the father of all who play the lyre and the pipe.'

viii. Shem is described as *ʾăḥî yepet*, 'Japheth's brother,' in 10:21; and *ʾāḥîw*, 'his brother' occurs in 4:21.

ix. The very word *šēm*, 'Shem,' in 10:21, is ubiquitous in 4:16–26, occurring in 4:17 (bis), 4:19 (bis), 4:21, 4:25, 4:26 (bis); the last attestation is the all important *šēm YHWH*, 'the name of Yahweh.'

Accordingly, this one little verse, 10:21, serves a major function in demonstrating the correlation between C and C′.

Finally, we may note one further parallel. Cassuto has noted that the number of descendants of Shem, Ham, and Japheth in 10:1–32 amounts to 71. If we exclude Nimrod who is special unto himself, we arrive at the figure 70 which is used in Canaanite and Israelite literature to describe a large brood or a complete family.[19]

[18] Cassuto, *From Noah to Abraham*, 217.
[19] Cassuto, *From Noah to Abraham*, 175–79.

This figure is important in its own right, but it becomes even more important in light of the relationship between 10:1–32 and 4:16–26. Before discussing the importance, first let us establish that there are indeed 70 descendants. We will list them by verse:

10:2 — Gomer, Magog, Madai, Javan, Tubal, Meshech, Tiras
10:3 — Ashkenaz, Riphath, Togarmah
10:4 — Elishah, Tarshish, Kittim, Dodanim
10:6 — Cush, Mizraim, Put, Canaan
10:7 — Seba, Havilah, Sabtah, Raamah, Sabteca, Sheba, Dedan
10:13 — Ludim, Anamim, Lehabim, Naphtuhim
10:14 — Pathrusim, Casluhim, Philistines, Caphtorim
10:15 — Sidon, Heth
10:16 — Jebusites, Amorites, Girgashites
10:17 — Hivites, Arkites, Sinites
10:18 — Arvadites, Zemarites, Hamathites
10:22 — Elam, Asshur, Arpachshad, Lud, Aram
10:23 — Uz, Hul, Gether, Mash
10:24 — Shelah, Eber
10:25 — Peleg, Joktan
10:26 — Almodad, Sheleph, Hazarmaveth, Jerah
10:27 — Hadoram, Uzal, Diklah
10:28 — Obal, Abimael, Sheba
10:29 — Ophir, Havilah, Jobab

There are, as exegetes have noted, duplicates in the list, e.g., Havilah in 10:7 and 10:29, Asshur in 10:11 and 10:22, Sheba in 10:7 and 10:28, etc., and Cush in 10:6–8 seems to refer to three distinct places,[20] but there are nonetheless 70 descendants of Noah's three sons in C′. This figure recalls the two numbers appearing in Lamech's song in 4:24, 7 and 77, and is moreover the difference between them. The numbers 7, 70, and 77 are obviously common in biblical literature, but their use in C and C′ cannot be coincidental. They were intentionally included to further illuminate the relationship between these two sections.

[20] Sasson, "Redactional Structuring," 212, n 3.

D TEN GENERATIONS FROM ADAM TO NOAH (5:1–32)

D′ TEN GENERATIONS FROM NOAH TO TERAH (11:10–26)

These two units within the Primeval History are universally recognized as being parallel.[21] In D we are given the ten generations Adam-Seth-Enosh-Kenan-Mahalalel-Jared-Enoch-Methusaleh-Lamech-Noah. In D′ we are given the ten generations (Noah-)Shem-Arpachshad-Shelah-Eber-Peleg-Reu-Serug-Nahor-Terah. The first list ends with the notice of Noah's *three* sons, Shem, Ham, and Japheth. The second list ends with the notice of Terah's *three* sons, Abram, Nahor, and Haran. In each case, the most important of the three sons is listed in primary position. Each genealogical list presents us with exceptionally long life-spans, though of course those in D′ are much shorter than those in D. And finally, in accord with our comparison of A and A′, 5:1–2 refers to Creation and 11:10 refers to the Flood.

D′ is the only unit which is out of order within the redactional structuring. But since it brings human history down to the personage of Abram, the compiler really had no choice but to place it after E′. This will be discussed a bit further in the next section.

E DOWNFALL: THE NEPHILIM (6:1–8)

E′ DOWNFALL: THE TOWER OF BABEL (11:1–9)

Apart from recognizing a redactional structuring in the entire Primeval History, the most important contribution of Sasson's seminal article was its adducing the parallels between these two narratives.[22] The episode of the

[21] Davidson, *Genesis 1–11*, 109; Sarna, *Understanding Genesis*, 43–44; and Cassuto, *From Noah to Abraham*, 250.

[22] Sasson, "Redactional Structuring," especially 216–19. For another attempt to place the Nephilim episode within the greater setting

Nephilim follows Creation, the strife between Adam's sons, and the technological development of mankind. The Tower of Babel story follows the Flood, the strife among Noah's sons, and the ethnic development of mankind. E and E′ deal chiefly with mankind's hubris which leads to God's intervention in human affairs.

The two stories have a number of theme-words which further link them together.

i. Each episode begins with *wayᵉhî*, in 6:1 and 11:1, the only two units in the Primeval History to do so (though B′ does begin with plural *wayyīhᵉyû*).

ii. *hēḥēl*, 'began,' occurs in 6:1; and *haḥillām*, 'their beginning,' occurs in 11:6.

iii. The phrase *ʿal pᵉnê hâʾădāmâ*, 'on the face of the soil,' appears in 6:1 and 6:7; and the phrase *ʿal pᵉnê kol hâʾāreṣ*, 'on the face of all the earth,' appears in 11:4, 11:8, 11:9.

iv. The word *lāhem*, 'to them, for them,' occurs repeatedly in both stories, in 6:1, 6:2, 6:4, and in 11:3 (bis).

v. In 6:2 and 6:4 we have *bᵉnê hâʾĕlōhîm*, 'sons of the gods' (= the pantheon), and *bᵉnôt hāʾādām*, 'the daughters of men'; in 11:5 we have *bānû bᵉnê hāʾādām*, 'the sons of man built,' in 11:8 we have *libnōt*, 'to build,' and in 11:4 we have *nibneh*, 'let us build.' In other words, the two expressions in E are more or less combined in E′ into *bᵉnê hāʾādām*, and E′ also presents us with three occurrences of the root *bnh*. Whether or not the root is etymologically related to "son, daughter" is irrelevant,[23] for in the Hebrew ear they no doubt were assonant.

vi. The protagonists in E are referred to as *ʾanšê haššēm*, literally 'men of the name' (= men of renown), in 6:4; the protagonists in E′ state *wᵉnaʿăśeh llānû šēm*, 'and so make a name for ourselves,' in 11:4. The word *šēm*, 'name,' is a key theme-word linking the two units for

---

of the Primeval History, see D. J. A. Clines, "The Significance of the 'Sons of God' Episode (Genesis 6:1–4) in the Context of the 'Primeval History' (Genesis 1–11)," *JSOT* 13 (1979) 33–46.

[23] See the discussion in BDB, 119–20.

it more than any other point illustrates the hubris central to both episodes.[24]

vii. *wayyar*ʾ *YHWH*, 'Yahweh saw,' occurs in 6:5, halfway through E; and *wayyēred YHWH lirʾōt*, 'Yahweh came down to see,' occurs in 11:5, midway through E'.

viii. The root *ʿśh* 'make, do,' is used twice in 6:6–7 and twice in 11:6.

There are also other points which are parallel in the Nephilim episode and the Tower of Babel story.

ix. The words *lārōb*, 'to be great, to multiply,' in 6:1 and *rabbâ*, 'great,' in 6:5, are conspicuous in E; their opposites *ʾeḥāt*, 'one,' and *ʾăḥādîm*, 'few,' in 11:1, and *ʾeḥād*, 'one' in 11:6, are conspicuous in E'.

x. The Nephilim myth ends with a wordplay in 6:6–8 with *wayyinnāḥem*, 'was sorry,' *niḥamtî*, 'I am sorry,' *nōaḥ*, 'Noah,' and *ḥēn*, 'favor';[25] the Tower of Babel narrative ends with a famous wordplay in 11:7–9 with *nābᵉlâ*, 'let us confuse,' *bābel*, 'Babel,' and *bālal*, 'confused.'

xi. The divine name Yahweh occurs five times in each unit.

xii. The Nephilim story relates how the gods came down to the human realm; and the Tower of Babel story tells of man's efforts to reach the divine realm (see 11:4 *wᵉrôʾšô baššāmayim*, 'with its head in the heavens').

These four points of contact together with the eight shared theme-words above demonstrate the relationship between E and E', thus supporting in greater detail the suggestion forwarded by Sasson several years ago.

Attention to redactional structuring aided us in solving two exegetical problems above, and now a third question may also be answered. The matter in dispute is whether 6:5–8 is functionally part of what precedes it, the Nephilim myth in 6:1–4, or part of what follows, the

24 Already hinted at by Fishbane (*Text and Texture*, 39).

25 The anagram in these last two words is noted by Cassuto (*From Adam to Noah*, 307).

Flood epic in 6:9–9:17. Commentators such as John Skinner,[26] E. A. Speiser,[27] and C. A. Simpson,[28] and translations such as the New American Bible and the Jerusalem Bible consider 6:5–8 to be part of the Flood story, while Sasson[29] and Michael Fishbane[30] argue that it belongs to the Nephilim fragment. Because a number of elements in these verses are linked to the Tower of Babel story, we are able to side with the latter group and regard 6:5–8 to be an integral part of E. We might also note that this accords with the rabbinic division of the Torah since 6:8 concludes the portion of Bereshit and 6:9 commences the portion of Noaḥ.

As stated earlier, whereas the Downfall of E follows the Ten Generations of D, the Downfall of E′ precedes the Ten Generations of D′. This makes the structure of the Primeval History slightly imperfect, but the redactor was left with no choice. Since D′ ends with Terah's fathering of Abram, this has to end the Primeval History and pave the way for the Abraham Cycle of 11:27–22:24. To end the Primeval History with the Tower of Babel story would have yielded a perfect structure, but the compiler sacrificed this goal for a more sensible continuity.

OVERVIEW

There can be little doubt that the structure of the Primeval History set forth in the above pages was deliberately produced by the redactor of Genesis. Too many overall themes, general story links, key vocabulary items, and other details are shared by A and A′, B and B′, C and C′, D and D′, and E and E′ for the structure of 1:1–11:26 to be coincidental. We can reaffirm Sasson's discovery of

[26] J. Skinner, *Genesis* (New York, 1910) 147–51.

[27] Speiser, *Genesis*, 44–56.

[28] C. A. Simpson, "Genesis," *The Interpreter's Bible* I (New York, 1952) 536–39.

[29] Sasson, "Redactional Structuring," 216.

[30] Fishbane, *Text and Texture*, 30–33.

several years ago that "the episodes culled from Hebraic traditions of early history were conceived in two matching sequences."

The midway point, or focus, of the Primeval History is 6:8–9 proclaiming Noah as a righteous man who found favor with Yahweh. The cycle in 1:1–11:26 hinges on this fact. Everything from 1:1–6:8 shows the gradual trend from *ṭôb*, 'good' (1:4), to *ra*ᶜ, 'bad' (6:5), culminating with the hope personified by Noah (6:8). It will be Noah with whom God makes the covenant. Everything from 6:9–11:26 repeats the first sequence, showing the trend from *ṣaddîq*, 'righteous' (6:9) to *yāzᵉmû*, 'devising evil' (11:6), culminating with the hope personified by Abra(ha)m (11:26). It will be Abra(ha)m with whom God makes another covenant.

It is not coincidental that our focus is also the division between Parshat Bereshit and Parshat Noaḥ in the Jewish annual reading cycle. The rabbis who established this system had a keen sense of where one major section ended and another began. This holds not only for the first two portions of Genesis but, as we shall see in forthcoming chapters, for other parts as well.

Our redactor did not end his task with the simple alignment of the parallel episodes into the two matching sequences. He went further. He not only included theme-words and similar phrases which link each episode to its parallel member, but he also included vocabulary items which link each episode to its predecessor and successor. Normally, though not always, these catchwords occur within a few verses of each other, though in different units.[31]

Let us see how this technique is carried out. A ends with *wayᵉgāreš*, 'he banished,' in 3:24, which is echoed in B

[31] A similar technique has been pointed out by Fishbane (*Text and Texture*, 16, 19) for the sub-units which comprise A. Note *haššāmayim wᵉhāʾāreṣ*, 'heaven and earth,' in 2:4a and *ʾereṣ wᵉšāmāyim*, 'earth and heaven,' in 2:4b; and *ᶜărummîm*, 'naked,' in 2:25 and *ᶜārûm*, 'cunning,' in 3:1.

by *gērăštā*, 'you have banished,' in 4:14.[32] A key word in B is *šibᶜātayim*, 'sevenfold,' in 4:15 which reoccurs in C in 4:24. C ends with *wayyiqrā ᵓet šᵉmô ᵓĕnôš*, 'he called his name Enosh (= man),' in 4:26, and D begins with *wayyiqrā ᵓet šᵉmām ᵓādām*, 'he called his name Man,' in 5:2.[33] Throughout D there appears the phrase *wayyôled bānîm ûbānôt*, 'he bore sons and daughters,' and E begins with *ûbānôt yullᵉdû lāhem*, 'and daughters were born to them,' in 6:1.[34] E ends with *wᵉnōaḥ*, 'and Noah,' in 6:8, which is resumed in A′ by *nōaḥ*, 'Noah,' in 6:9, and both of these refer to Noah in a very positive manner.

Towards the end of A′ comes *ᵓet nōaḥ wᵉᵓet bānāw*, 'Noah and his sons,' in 9:1, and B′ begins with *bᵉnê nōaḥ*, 'sons of Noah,' in 9:18. B′ ends with *kol yᵉmê nōaḥ*, 'all the days of Noah,' in 9:29, which is echoed at the start of C′ by *tôlᵉdôt bᵉnê nōaḥ*, 'the generations of the sons of Noah,' in 10:1. Peculiar to C′ is *lilšōnô*, 'according to its language,' in 10:5, and *lilšōnōtām*, 'according to their languages,' in 10:20, 10:31, which reverberates at the start of E′ with *śāpâ ᵓeḥāt*, 'one tongue,' in 11:1. Finally *šēm*, 'name,' in 11:4, is central to E′, and *šēm*, 'Shem,' appears in 11:10 at the head of the genealogical list which comprises D′. It might be noted that although the redactor was forced to place E′ before D′, he still was able to use catchwords which bridge C′ and E′ ('language' and 'tongue') and E′ and D′ (*šēm*).

We can conclude this chapter by marveling at the brilliant structure which pervades the Primeval History. To summarize: 1) parallel episodes are aligned in matching sequence; 2) story lines, themes, theme-words, and

[32] Actually there are numerous nexuses linking the Garden of Eden episode in 3:1–24 with the Cain and Abel account in 4:1–16; see Fishbane, *Text and Texture*, 26–27.

[33] Cassuto (*From Adam to Noah*, 276) seems to point this out, but not clearly.

[34] Cassuto (*From Adam to Noah*, 219) points this out also, calling it "an obvious nexus."

other details highlight the rapport between parallel episodes; 3) the pivot in 6:8–9 focuses on Noah and is in accord with the rabbinic division of the Primeval History; and 4) nexuses connect each successive unit.

II

THE ABRAHAM CYCLE

The Primeval History ends at 11:26 with the mention of Terah's progeny, and the very next verse begins what we term the Abraham Cycle. In 1:1–11:26 the concern is universalistic; from 11:27 on the concern is particularistic. The events described in the Primeval History befell all mankind. The succeeding chapters will focus on one small subset of mankind, the people Israel, and the story of that nation begins with Abraham, its first patriarch.

The standard view regarding the Abraham Cycle is that "the various stories are but loosely connected. Almost any one, with the possible exception of the stories of the call of Abraham and of the sacrifice of Isaac, might have been omitted without having seriously impaired the unity of the Abraham story as a whole, and without our being conscious that anything was lacking."[1] But such is not the case, for a redactional structuring similar to that discussed in chap. I is also forthcoming in the Abraham Cycle.

Every commentator on Genesis has remarked on the duplication of 12:10–20 and 20:1–18 (as well as the triplicate in 26:6–11). Many scholars have also pointed out similarities between 12:1–9 and 22:1–19, for they are the two episodes central to Abraham's life as specifically mentioned in the above quotation. But it was not until among the last words ever penned by the great savant, U. Cassuto, that all the Abraham stories were seen as

[1] J. Morgenstern, *The Book of Genesis* (New York, 1965) 188.

duplicates of one another. Cassuto spoke of ten trials or ordeals which Abraham undergoes[2] and wrote as follows:

> Note should also be taken of the chiastic parallelism between the ten episodes. The last trial corresponds to the first. (*Go from your country* etc.; *and go to the land of Moriah* etc.; in the former passage there is the command to leave his father, in the latter to bid farwell [*sic*] to his son; in both episodes the blessings and promises are similar in content and in phrasing). The penultimate two tests parallel the pair of tests following the first (in the earlier trials Sarai is in danger from Pharaoh, and Lot goes away; in the later ordeals Sarah's peril stems from Abimelech, and Hagar and Ishmael depart; in both sets of tests a sanctuary is founded and the name of the Lord is proclaimed). The seventh episode corresponds to the fourth (in both Lot is in jeopardy and is saved). Similarly, the sixth trial parallels the fifth (both appertain to Ishmael and Isaac).[3]

In this chapter, the basic structure outlined by Cassuto is accepted. It was not our privilege to see the master's work completed, so we have no idea how far he would have carried forth and built on this foundation. In the pages that follow many details are set forth which sustain Cassuto's schema. Two controls in the Abraham Cycle, to be discussed below, act as a litmus test and point to the fundamental accuracy of his proposal. Finally, I expand Cassuto's structure to include the individual units immediately preceding and following the ten ordeals.

The structure of 11:27–22:24 is therefore as follows:

A Genealogy of Terah (11:27–32)
B Start of Abram's Spiritual Odyssey (12:1–9)
C Sarai in foreign palace; ordeal ends in peace and success; Abram and Lot part (12:10–13:18)
D Abram comes to the rescue of Sodom and Lot (14:1–24)

[2] Abraham's ten trials are already referred to in rabbinic literature, most prominently in Avot 5:4. See also the sources cited by L. Ginzberg, *The Legends of the Jews* V (Philadelphia, 1953) 218, n 52.

[3] U. Cassuto, *From Noah to Abraham* (Jerusalem, 1964) 296. The quotation comes from an appendix to this work, a fragment of Part Three of the author's commentary on Genesis.

E Covenant with Abram; Annunciation of Ishmael (15:1–16:16)
E′ Covenant with Abraham; Annunciation of Isaac (17:1–18:15)
D′ Abraham comes to the rescue of Sodom and Lot (18:16–19:38)
C′ Sarah in foreign palace; ordeal ends in peace and success; Abraham and Ishmael part (20:1–21:34)
B′ Climax of Abraham's Spiritual Odyssey (22:1–19)
A′ Genealogy of Nahor (22:20–24)

In the Primeval History the redactional structuring was built along parallel lines. Five episodes (A, B, C, D, E) occur and are then repeated, with one necessary exception, in matching order (A′, B′, C′, E′, D′). In the Abraham Cycle a different system is used, one which Cassuto labels "chiastic parallelism." Five units are included (A, B, C, D, E) and are then duplicated in reverse order (E′, D′, C′, B′, A′). As was done in chap. I, let us proceed to an analysis of each of the matching pairs.

A GENEALOGY OF TERAH (11:27–32)
A′ GENEALOGY OF NAHOR (22:20–24)

These two units act as bookends for the Abraham Cycle, encasing the essential events in the life of the first patriarch. In the first one the family of Abraham's father, Terah, is discussed. In the second one the family of Abraham's brother, Nahor, is treated. Three points further link the two genealogies.

i. In 11:27, one important grandchild, Lot, is mentioned, and he is the offspring of the last-named son, Haran. In 22:23, one important grandchild, Rebekah, is mentioned, and she is the offspring of the last-named son (of the primary wife), Bethuel. In both cases, this grandchild will play a prominent role in the chapters that follow.[4]

[4] On the introduction of Lot and Rebekah in these genealogies, see N. M. Sarna, "The Anticipatory Use of Information as a Literary Feature of the Genesis Narratives," in *The Creation of Sacred Literature* (ed. R. E. Friedman; Berkeley, 1981) 78–80.

ii. In 11:29 a character otherwise not central to the narratives is introduced with the word *ʾăbî*, namely, *ʾăbî yiskâ*, 'father of Iscah.' In 22:21, the same phenomenon occurs with *ʾăbî ʾărām*, 'father of Aram.' But in each case there is a rationale for mentioning the character. In 11:29 Iscah is introduced to inform us that Nahor's father-in-law Haran is not the same individual as his brother Haran.[5] In 22:21 we learn of Aram because of the prominent place Paddan Aram and Aram Naharaim will have in the Jacob Cycle.[6]

iii. In 11:30 we read of the childless Sarai whom we are to contrast with the very fertile Milcah and Reumah in 22:20–24.

Scholars have wondered why the Nahor genealogy was placed in its present position. Gerhard von Rad wrote, "The section is told as an event in Abraham's life (v. 20). But one can see immediately that an Aramean genealogy exists here, which is incorporated artlessly into the biographical context of the narrative."[7] By recognizing the redactional structuring in the Abraham Cycle we are able to discover the compiler's mastery and see 22:20–24 as the matching bookend to 11:27–32. Far from being carried out "artlessly," the redactor has performed his task brilliantly and artistically.

B START OF ABRAM'S SPIRITUAL ODYSSEY (12:1–9)

B′ CLIMAX OF ABRAHAM'S SPIRITUAL ODYSSEY (22:1–19)

Not only Cassuto but other commentators as well have noted the relationship between these two sections.[8]

[5] Cassuto, *From Noah to Abraham*, 277.

[6] Sarna, "The Anticipatory Use of Information as a Literary Feature of the Genesis Narratives," 80.

[7] G. von Rad, *Genesis* (Philadelphia, 1961) 240.

[8] N. M. Sarna, *Understanding Genesis* (New York, 1966) 160–61; R. Davidson, *Genesis 12–50* (Cambridge, 1979) 94; and B. Jacob, *Das erste Buch der Tora: Genesis* (Berlin, 1934) 493.

Most prominent among these is Nahum Sarna, whose term "spiritual odyssey" is here adopted. He recognized the following eight parallels and theme-words shared by B and B′:[9]

i. 12:1–9 marks the first occasion on which God speaks to Abram; and 22:1–19 is appropriately the last such occasion.

ii. In 12:1 God says *lek lᵉkā . . . ʾel hāʾāreṣ ʾăšer ʾarʾekā*, 'go forth . . . to the land which I will show you'; in 22:2 God says *lek lᵉkā ʾel ʾereṣ hammôriyyâ . . . ʾăšer ʾômar ʾēlekā*, 'go forth to the land of Moriah . . . which I will point out to you.'[10]

iii. In each instance, the exact destination of the patriarch's journey is unknown.

iv. Descriptive epithets are accumulated to heighten the tension of the drama. In 12:1 we read *mêʾarṣᵉkā ûmimmôladtᵉkā ûmibbêt ʾābîkā*, 'from your land, from your homeland, and from your father's house'; and in 22:2 we read *ʾet binkā ʾet yᵉḥîdkā ʾăšer ʾāhabtā ʾet yiṣḥāq*, 'your son, your favorite, Isaac whom you love.' In each case, the second person masculine singular pronoun suffix *-kā* or *-tā* is used three times to direct our attention further to Abraham.

v. In B father and son leave each other; in B′ father and son were prepared to see each other for the last time. The former represents a break with the past; the latter with the future.[11]

vi. In 12:6 Abram's journey takes him to *môreh* and in 22:2 the destination is *môriyyâ*.[12]

vii. In 12:7 we have *wayyiben šām mizbēaḥ laYHWH*, 'he built there an altar to Yahweh'; and in 22:9 we have *wayyiben šām ʾabrāhām ʾet hammizbēaḥ*, 'Abraham built there the altar.'

[9] Sarna, *Understanding Genesis*, 160–61.

[10] Jacob (*Das erste Buch der Tora: Genesis*, 493) also discusses the use of *lek lᵉkā* in these two contexts.

[11] As noted by Jacob (*Das erste Buch der Tora: Genesis*, 493) and Davidson (*Genesis 12–50*, 94).

[12] As Cassuto (*From Noah to Abraham*, 327) notes, the LXX translates both terms, whatever their designations, with the same word ὑψηλήν, 'high.' Were the Septuagint translators trying to show the relationship between the two stories?

viii. The blessings given to Abraham in B and B′ are strikingly similar. In 12:2 we have *w^{e}ʾeʿeśkâ l^{e}gôy gādôl*, 'I will make you a great nation'; and in 22:17 we read *w^{e}harbāh ʾarbeh ʾet zarʿăkā*, 'I will exceedingly multiply your seed.' In 12:2 we have *waʾăbārek^{e}kā . . . b^{e}rākâ*, 'I will bless you . . . a blessing'; and in 22:17 we read *bārēk ʾăbārek^{e}kā*, 'I will abundantly bless you.' In 12:3 we have *ûm^{e}qallelkā ʾāʾōr*, 'those who curse you I will curse'; and in 22:17 we read *w^{e}yîraš zarʿăkâ ʾēt šaʿar ʾōybāw*, 'your seed shall inherit the gate of its enemies.' And finally, in 12:3 we have *w^{e}nibr^{e}kû b^{e}kā kōl mišp^{e}ḥōt haʾădāmâ*, 'all the families of the earth will be blessed through you'; and in 22:18 we read *w^{e}hitbār^{e}kû b^{e}zarʿăkā kōl gôyê hāʾāreṣ*, 'all the nations of the earth will be blessed through your seed.'[13]

Still other correspondences between these two pericopes may be seen.

ix. 12:4 states *wayyēlek ʾittô lôṭ*, 'Lot went with him'; and 22:6, 22:8 state *wayyēl^{e}kû š^{e}nêhem yaḥdāw*, 'the two of them went on together.'

x. *wayyiqqaḥ*, 'he (Abra[ha]m) took,' occurs in 12:5 and 22:3.

xi. 12:5 refers to *ʾet hannepeš ʾăšer ʿāśû b^{e}ḥārān*, 'the people he acquired in Haran'; two of whom are presumably *ʾet š^{e}nê n^{e}ʿārāw*, 'the two servants,' in 22:3.

xii. *m^{e}qôm*, 'place,' occurs in 12:6; and *hammāqôm*, 'the place,' appears in 22:3–4. More significantly, the word is used with the connotation 'hallowed site' in both instances.[14]

xiii. *š^{e}kem*, 'Shechem,' is prominent in B, in 12:6; and this is echoed in B′ with the verb *wayyaškēm*, 'he arose,' in 22:3.

xiv. The appearance of God to Abram in B is significant, as with *wayyērāʾ YHWH ʾel ʾabrām*, 'Yahweh appeared

[13] Cassuto (*From Noah to Abraham*, 296–97) also notes that, not coincidentally, these two blessings each contain seven expressions of benison.

[14] See S. R. Driver, *The Book of Genesis* (London, 1905), 146; E. A. Speiser, *Genesis* (Garden City, NY, 1964) 86; Jacob, *Das erste Buch der Tora: Genesis*, 341; and BDB, 880, who all regard 12:6 as 'hallowed site.'

to Abram,' in 12:7; God is then described later in the verse as *hannirʾeh ʾēlāw*, 'who appeared to him.' In B', in 22:14, Abraham names the place *YHWH yirʾeh*, 'Yahweh-yireh,' because *YHWH yêrāʾeh*, 'Yahweh appears.'

xv. B ends with Abram traveling to the Negev and B' ends with Abraham dwelling in its most important city, Beersheba.

xvi. In B the words of God to Abram occur in two separate parts, in 12:1–3 and 12:7 with action described in the intervening verses. In B' the words of God to Abraham also occur separately, in 22:12 and 22:16–18 with action again described in the intervening verses. The word *wayyōʾmer*, 'he (God) said,' occurs before each speech, that is, twice in B and twice in B'. In each case, one speech is the conveyance of the blessing (12:1–3 and 22:16–18), and the other is a specific reference to the patriarch's offspring (*zarʿăkā*, 'your seed,' in 12:7 and *ʾet binkā ʾet yᵉhîdkā*, 'your son, your favorite,' in 22:12).

It is abundantly clear that the two stories are related. Numerous parallel themes and theme-words serve to connect them, alerting the reader to the literary texture of the Abraham Cycle. The redactor utilized these two episodes in the patriarch's life to mark the beginning and the end of his religious journey.

Attention to the redactional structuring in the Primeval History helped solve a number of thorny issues in biblical scholarship. Recognition of a similar structuring in the Abraham Cycle will likewise clarify some disputes. Many expositors of Genesis assert that 22:15–18 or 15-19 is a secondary addition to the episode describing Abraham's final test. Robert Davidson exemplifies the contention, "These verses are an appendix to the main narrative, somewhat artificially joined to it by claiming that

---

Cassuto (*From Noah to Abraham*, 323–24) denies this is intended in 12:6 but admits 'hallowed site' in 22:3–4.

the angel of the LORD spoke to Abraham *a second time* (verse 15)."[15] Von Rad proclaims, "It is clearly noticeable that the narrative once concluded with v. 14."[16]

In light of the redactional structuring in the Abraham Cycle, however, this position is untenable. Since B opens the Abraham Cycle (after the Terah genealogy) with God's blessing to the patriarch, B′ must close the Cycle (with only the Nahar genealogy to follow) with the same blessing. We have seen in point viii above that this is exactly the case. They are the most complete blessings of all those conveyed from God to Abraham, speaking of numerical increase, blessing in general, defeat of one's adversaries, and the patriarch as a source of blessing for others. And as mentioned in note 13, these blessings share the literary feature of seven separate expressions. In other words, given the opening blessing in 12:2–3, the closing blessing in 22:17–18 is demanded. Furthermore, in point xvi above it is noted that God speaks twice to Abra(ha)m in B and thus will be expected in B′ also.

The expectation of the concluding blessing in the Abraham Cycle is highlighted by the word *šēnit*, 'a second time,' in 22:15. The ten ordeals which Abraham undergoes are the build-up for the climactic blessing at the end of the Cycle. Accordingly, *šēnît* is used in Genesis exactly as in Jonah. Cyrus Gordon has pointed out that the prophet suffers through an ordeal, then the word *šēnît* appears in Jonah 3:1, and then "the fulfillment of his mission follows as the climax. The key to the structure of the Book is the adverb *šēnît*, 'a second time.'"[17] The same holds true for Genesis. Davidson, von Rad, et al. argue that *šēnît* in 22:15 is evidence for the secondary

[15] Davidson, *Genesis 12–50*, 97. See also Driver, *The Book of Genesis*, 220; Morgenstern, *The Book of Genesis*, 152; and J. Skinner, *Genesis* (New York, 1910) 331.

[16] Von Rad, *Genesis*, 237.

[17] C. H. Gordon, "Build-Up and Climax," *Studies in Bible and the Ancient Near East Presented to Samuel E. Loewenstamm* (ed. Y. Avishur and J. Blau; Jerusalem, 1978) 30.

nature of the verses which follow. On the contrary, as in Jonah, this word is central to the literary composition.[18]

C SARAI IN FOREIGN PALACE; ORDEAL ENDS IN PEACE AND SUCCESS; ABRAM AND LOT PART (12:10–13:18)

C′ SARAH IN FOREIGN PALACE; ORDEAL ENDS IN PEACE AND SUCCESS; ABRAHAM AND ISHMAEL PART (20:1–21:34)

The first *lek lᵉkā* episode is followed by the story of Sarai in Pharaoh's palace (12:10–20), an ordeal which ends in peace and success (13:1–4), and is then followed by the story of Abram's and Lot's parting (13:5–18). The second *lek lᵉkā* episode is preceded by a unit comprised of three corresponding pericopes. We have the story of Sarah in Abimelech's palace (20:1-18), the story of Abraham's and Ishmael's parting (21:1–21), and the conclusion of the Abimelech story leading to peace and success (21:22–34).[19]

C and C′ are thus divisible into three smaller sections. The foreign palace scenes we will call Ca and C′a, the peace and success scenes Cb and C′b, and the parting scenes Cc and C′c. It should be noted that whereas the order in 12:10–13:18 is Ca, Cb, Cc, the order in 20:1–21:34 is C′a, C′c, C′b. The reason for this arrangement will be discussed below. But first let us proceed to a discussion of the parallel details in each of the three subsections.

In Ca and C′a, which are universally recognized as duplicates, the following theme-words are shared.

i. In 12:11 we read *wayyōʾmer ʾel śāray ʾištô*, 'he said to Sarai his wife'; and in 20:2 we read *wayyōʾmer ʾabrāhām ʾel śārâ ʾištô*, 'Abraham said to Sarah his wife.'

[18] Jacob (*Das erste Buch der Tora: Genesis*, 502) correctly understood this.

[19] This is noted not only by Cassuto but by Sarna (*Understanding Genesis*, 161) too.

ii. Abra(ha)m's fear is voiced in 12:12 *wᵉhārᵉgû ᵓōtî*, 'they will kill me,' and in 20:11 *wahărāgûnî*, 'they will kill me.'
iii. The key word *ᵓăḥōtî*, 'my sister,' occurs in 12:13 and 20:2.
iv. Sarai/Sarah is referred to in both stories as *hâᵓiššâ*, 'the woman,' in 12:14–15 and 20:3.
v. The verbal root *lqḥ*, 'take,' occurs in 12:15 and 20:3–4.
vi. In each episode Abra(ha)m gains *ṣōᵓn ûbāqār*, 'flocks and herds,' and *ᶜăbādîm ûšᵉpāḥōt*, 'male and female slaves,' in 12:16 and 20:14.
vii. The verbal root *ngᶜ*, 'afflict, plague,' is used in 12:17; the same root but with the meaning 'touch' is used in 20:6.
viii. The words *ᶜal dᵉbar*, 'on account of,' appear in 12:17 and 20:11, 20:18.
ix. In 12:17 Sarai is called *ᵓēšet ᵓabrām*, 'Abram's wife'; and in 20:18 Sarah is called *ᵓēšet ᵓabrāhām*, 'Abraham's wife.'
x. In 12:18 we read *wayyiqrāᵓ parᶜōh lᵉᵓabrām wayyōᵓmer*, 'Pharaoh called to Abram and said'; in 20:9 we have *wayyiqrāᵓ ᵓăbîmelek lᵉᵓabrāhām wayyōᵓmer*, 'Abimelech called to Abraham and said.'
xi. *zōᵓt ᶜāśîtā*, 'this you did,' appears in 12:18; and *ᶜāśîtā zōᵓt*, 'you did this,' occurs in 20:6.
xii. The return of the patriarch's wife is heralded by the word *wᵉᶜattâ*, 'now,' in both 12:19 and 20:7.

The connections between Ca and C'a are obvious. In each Abra(ha)m tries to pass his wife off as his sister to save his own neck, Sarai/Sarah winds up in the palace of a foreign king, God intercedes, the wrath of the monarch is incurred, the patriarch's wife is returned, and Abra(ha)m leaves richer than when he entered. As if these parallels were not enough to alert the reader to the relationship between the two stories, the above twelve theme-words are also included.

Neither Cb nor C'b is very long and neither is very central to the patriarchal narratives. But even here there are links which point to their interconnection.

xiii. In 13:1 Abram heads for the Negev; and in 21:31 we gain an etymology for Beersheba, the region's most important city.

xiv. Among the patriarch's possessions in 13:2 is *miqneh*, 'livestock' and in 21:27 we read of his *ṣōʾn ûbāqār*, 'flocks and herds.'

xv. Most important of all, in 13:4 we have *wayyiqrāʾ šām ʾabrām bᵉšēm YHWH*, 'Abram invoked there the name of Yahweh'; and in 21:33 we have *wayyiqrāʾ šām bᵉšēm YHWH*, 'he (Abraham) invoked there the name of Yahweh.'

Here it should be noted that regard for redactional structuring alleviates the problem sensed by E. A. Speiser at 21:33. He wrote, "One can only guess at the reason why such a brief excerpt from *J* was inserted at this particular point."[20] Clearly, Abraham's invoking Yahweh in this verse was needed to balance the same action by the patriarch in 13:4.

The subsections Cc and C′c recount the separation of Abra(ha)m and one of his kinsmen. Again we may note parallels which link the two episodes.

xvi. Central to Abraham's and Lot's parting is the *rîb*, 'quarrel,' in 13:7; and a major point of Abraham's and Ishmael's parting is the latter becoming a *rôbeh*, 'archer,' in 21:20. The words are from different verbal roots, but the assonance is undeniable.

xvii. In 13:10 we read *wayyiśśāʾ lôṭ ʾet ʿênāw wayyarʾ*, 'Lot lifted up his eyes and saw'; and in 21:19 we have *wayyipqaḥ ʾĕlōhîm ʾet ʿênehā wattēreʾ*, 'God opened up her eyes and she saw.'

xviii. The word *miṣrayim*, 'Egypt,' is cleverly included in 13:10 because it appears in 21:21 too.

xix. The word *zarʿăkā*, 'your seed,' obtains in both 13:15–16 and 21:13.

xx. God promises Abram *wᵉśamtî ʾet zarʿăkā kaʿăpar hāʾāreṣ*, 'I will make your seed like the dust of the earth,' in 13:16; and he promises Hagar *lᵉgôy gādôl ʾăśîmennû*, 'I will make him a great nation,' in 21:18.

xxi. In 13:14–17 the patriarch receives the land of Canaan; in 21:1–7 he receives his son Isaac who is then cir-

[20] Speiser, *Genesis*, 160.

> cumcised. The land and Isaac are inextricably intertwined throughout the patriarchal narratives,[21] and the land and circumcision are specifically collocated at the establishment of the covenant in 17:8–10.

It might be objected that a good portion of C′c is concerned with the birth, circumcision, and weaning of Isaac, happenings which have no apparent parallel in Cc. But the major push in 21:1–7 is not the birth of Isaac as a birth story. In the patriarchal narratives the annunciations, not the births, are the important factor, for they dominate 16:7–14, 18:9–15, 25:21–23. The births themselves receive very little attention, as witness 16:15–16, 21:1–3, 25:24–26. So even as important an event as Isaac's birth need not a priori have as its parallel Ishmael's birth in the redactional structure. As we shall see below, their annunciations are parallel, but not their births. The parallel to Isaac's birth, then, as noted in point xxi above, is Abram's acquisition of Canaan in 13:4–7. Furthermore, Isaac's appearance is used to elicit a conflict which leads to Ishmael's leaving, just as a conflict caused Lot's separation.

Next we must address the question why the order is Ca, Cb, Cc in 12:10–13:18 but C′a, C′c, C′b in 20:1–21:34. Or, in other words, why does the story of Ishmael's and Abraham's separation (21:1–21) precede the verses dealing with Abraham's success which culminates in his invoking Yahweh (21:22–34)? After all, in the corresponding subsections, the story of Lot's and Abram's parting (13:5–18), follows the discourse on Abram's success culminating in his invoking Yahweh (13:1–4). The answer is twofold, and the clues come from the passages just before C′c and just after C′b. The verses immediately preceding 21:1–21 read as follows: "Abraham interceded with God, and God healed Abimelech, that is, his wife and his maidservants, so that they could bear children. For Yahweh had closed fast every womb in Abimelech's household on account of Sarah, Abraham's wife" (20:17–18). The very next verses

[21] See the acute observations of Sarna (*Understanding Genesis*, 171–72).

tell of Yahweh's taking note of Sarah and how she too bore a child (21:1–2). By placing the story of Ishmael's leaving, which begins with Isaac's birth, before the story of Abraham's success, the compiler achieved a juxtaposition whereby 20:17–18 and 21:1–2 both describe the opening of wombs, both somehow connected with God, Abraham, and Sarah.

Secondly, there is a need for the passage of time between 21:1–21, where Isaac is but a baby, and 22:1–19, where Isaac is grown up. Note that he is able to speak, walk, carry wood, and understand what comprises a sacrifice. By interposing the story of Abraham's success, the redactor neatly accomplished his goal of separating these two events in the life of Isaac. In short, by switching the order of C′c and C′b, the compiler 1) made the two passages dealing with opening the womb contiguous, and 2) allowed for the passage of time between Isaac the infant and Isaac the grown lad.

D ABRAM COMES TO THE RESCUE OF SODOM AND LOT (14:1–24)

D′ ABRAHAM COMES TO THE RESCUE OF SODOM AND LOT (18:16–19:38)

Following C and preceding C′ are two units which both tell of the patriarch's intervention into the affairs of Sodom leading to the rescue of his nephew Lot. The story lines are undoubtedly analogous, but to drive home this point we are as usual presented with numerous shared theme-words.

i. The king of Sodom in 14:2 is *bera*^{c} which, whether or not intended by the author, can be read 'in evil'; the root *r*^{c} (more properly *r*^{cc}), 'evil,' occurs in 19:7, 19:9, 19:19.

ii. Similarly, the king of Gomorrah in 14:2 is *birša*^{c} which, again whether intended or not, can be read 'in wickedness'; the word *rāšā*^{c}, 'wicked,' occurs in 18:23, 18:25 (bis).

iii. The place name *ṣōᶜar* appears as a gloss in 14:2, 14:8; and we gain an etymology for it in 19:22.
iv. The word *melaḥ*, 'salt,' is used in both 14:3 and 19:26.
v. To escape danger the people of the Pentapolis *herâ nāsû*, 'fled to the hills,' in 14:10; and in 19:19–20 we see the same stems used *hāhārâ . . . lānûs*, 'to the hills . . . to flee.'
vi. *happālîṭ*, 'the refugee,' is used in 14:13; and the like-sounding, semantically close *himmālēṭ*, 'to escape,' is used in 19:17 (bis), 19:19, 19:22 (see also *ᵓimmālᵉṭâ*, 'let me escape,' in 19:20).
vii. In 14:13 we learn that Abram is in *ᵓēlōnê mamrēᵓ*; when 18:33 is read with 18:1 we learn that the patriarch is in the same locale in this chapter.
viii. *hāᶜām*, 'the people,' is used to refer to the general Sodomite population in 14:16 and 19:4.
ix. Melchizedek's name in 14:18 includes the element *ṣedeq*, 'righteousness'; and the same root occurs in *ṣᵉdāqâ*, 'righteousness,' in 18:19 and in *ṣaddîq*, 'righteous,' in 18:23–28 (seven times).
x. In 14:18 we read of a meal comprised of bread and wine; and in 19:3 drink and baked goods are similarly served.
xi. In 14:19 we have *bārûk ᵓabrām*, 'blessed be Abram'; and in 18:18 we have *wᵉnibrᵉkû bô*, 'they will be blessed through him (Abraham).'
xii. God is called *qônēh šāmayim wāᵓāreṣ*, 'creator of heaven and earth,' in 14:19, 14:22; and his power over these natural forces is rehearsed in 19:23–24 where the sun sets *ᶜal hāᵓāreṣ*, 'upon the earth,' and brimstone and fire descend *min haššāmayim*, 'from the heavens.'
xiii. Abram gives *maᶜăśēr*, 'one-tenth,' to Melchizedek in 14:20; and the negotiations with God end at *ᶜăśārâ*, 'ten (men),' in 18:32.

Again we are able to solve a literary critical problem by paying heed to the redactional structure in the Abraham Cycle. Some scholars[22] have been plagued by the appearance of *min haššāmayim*, 'from the heavens,' in 19:24, for it seems unnecessary and clumsy. But it is specifically

[22] Skinner, *Genesis*, 309; *BHS*, ad loc.; and *NAB*, ad loc.

placed near *hāʾāreṣ*, 'the earth,' in 19:23, to evoke the epithet *qônēh šāmayim wāʾāreṣ*, 'creator of heaven and earth,' in 14:19, 14:22, as noted above in point xii. Without the references to heaven in 19:24 the balance would be incomplete. Moreover, it is specifically Yahweh who is present in 19:23–24, just as he is included in 14:22.

E COVENANT WITH ABRAM; ANNUNCIATION OF ISHMAEL (15:1–16:16)

E′ COVENANT WITH ABRAHAM; ANNUNCIATION OF ISAAC (17:1–18:15)

Standing at the center of the Abraham Cycle are two parallel units describing the covenant established between God and the patriarch and the annunciation of a son in fulfillment of that covenant. As with C and C′, these two units can be neatly divided into subsections. The covenant portions, 15:1–21 and 17:1–27, we will label Ea and E′a;[23] and the annunciation scenes, 16:1–16 and 18:1–15, we will label Eb and E′b. The corresponding subsections will be compared separately, beginning with the two covenant chapters.

Scholars are quick to point out the differences between the two covenant narrations,[24] but as the following will attempt to demonstrate, in actuality they are related more closely than usually is admitted. Not only are several theme-words shared by the two chapters, but more importantly the exact order of action, ideas, and motifs is followed in Ea and E′a.

i. Each scene begins with God's appearance to Abra(ha)m, one using the noun *maḥăzeh*, 'vision,' in 15:1, the other the verb *wayyērāʾ*, 'appeared,' in 17:1.

ii. In each scene, God begins his speech to Abra(ha)m with mention of divine protection; in 15:1 we have

[23] For an attempt at seeing 17:1–27 itself as having been composed along chiastic lines, see S. E. McEvenue, *The Narrative Style of the Priestly Writer* (Rome, 1971) 157–58.

[24] Von Rad, *Genesis*, 192–93; and Speiser, *Genesis*, 126.

ānōkî māgēn lāk, 'I am your shield'; and in 17:1 we have *hithallēk lᵉpānay*, 'walk before me.' That the latter expression connotes divine protection may be determined from Ps 116:8–9.[25]

iii. Next God progresses to speak of reward and increase; 15:1 uses *śᵉkārkā harbēh mᵉʾōd*, 'your reward will be very great'; and 17:2 states *wᵉʾarbeh ʾôtkā bimʾōd mᵉʾōd*, 'I will make you exceedingly great.'

iv. In 15:3 Abram complains he is not a father *hēn lî lōʾ nātattā zāraᶜ*, 'but you have given me no offspring'; and in 17:4 a perfect corollary appears *wᵉhāyîtā lᵉʾab hămôn gôyîm*, 'you will be the father of a multitude of nations.'

v. E goes on to speak of many offspring in 15:4–5, with the specific use of *yēṣēʾ mimmēᶜekā*, 'will issue from your loins'; similarly E′ promises many offspring in 17:6, and specifically uses *mimmᵉkā yēṣēʾû*, 'from you will issue.'

vi. Next the land of Canaan is promised as an inheritance, in 15:7 and 17:8.

vii. Each pericope then proceeds to the description of a ceremony; in 15:9–11 it is the peculiar animals ritual and in 17:10–14 it is the circumcision ritual.

viii. In 15:13 a second communication from God to Abram commences with *wayyōʾmer lᵉʾabrām*, 'he said to Abram'; and in 17:15 God also begins a second speech to the patriarch with *wayyōʾmer ʾĕlōhîm ʾel ʾabrāhām*, 'God said to Abraham.'

ix. This second communication deals further with the promised offspring, in both 15:13–16 and 17:15–22.

x. The two episodes close with the completion of the ceremony described earlier, marked by *bên haggᵉzārîm*, 'between the pieces,' in 15:17 and the verb *mwl*, 'circumcise,' in 17:23–27.

There are naturally differences between the two covenants, in the names of the deity, the names of the patriarch, the rituals utilized, etc. And if one wanted to emphasize these differences, one could easily set up major distinctions between the two chapters. But as the above

[25] As astutely noted by Davidson, *Genesis 12–50*, 57; see also Jacob, *Das erste Buch der Tora: Genesis*, 419.

has shown, it is just as easy to show the striking similarities between them. With the possible exception of B and B′, no two episodes in the Abraham Cycle are as parallel as Ea and E′a. For in these two we have not only similar use of language, but perfectly parallel sequences of thought, speech, and action.[26] Within the Abraham Cycle, therefore, the paired units with the most affinities for each other are the start and climax of the patriarch's spiritual odyssey and the two covenants. This may be by design, for these episodes are by far the most important within the collection of stories which comprise the Cycle.

It is apposite to quote Gerhard von Rad on these sections. Concerning 15:1–21 he states a "certain characteristic is that the 'chief joint' in a text filled with joints occurs between v.6 and v.7" and that "there are too many contradictions in this chapter for one to think of it as an organic narrative unit."[27] Regarding 17:1–27 he writes that "it does not have a unified structure and continuity. A series of seams can be recognized, from which one concludes a successive combination of various Priestly traditions about the covenant with Abraham into a large unit."[28] This is not the point to enter into a detailed discussion of source criticism (see below chap. VI), but it should be noted here that von Rad's comments do not stand up to the findings of redactional structuring. If we had only 15:1–21 before us, we might agree that the chapter is a composite one, "filled with joints." Likewise if we possessed only 17:1–27 we might conclude that various traditions have been fused into one chapter. But the two covenant stories together seem to contravene von Rad's analysis.

For example, he saw a "chief joint" between 15:6, which ends a discussion of Abram's descendants, and 15:7, which grants the patriarch the land of Canaan. But

[26] Davidson (*Genesis 12–50*, 54–56) is one commentator who is partly aware of this.

[27] Von Rad, *Genesis*, 177.

[28] Von Rad, *Genesis*, 192.

in the corresponding unit, 17:7–8 inextricably links the descendants and the land, as von Rad readily admits.[29] If we see the two covenant stories as matching sequences, it cannot follow that 15:6 and 15:7 are to be separated. Descendants and land go hand-in-hand in E′a and accordingly are inseparable in Ea.

We may cite another example. Von Rad posits that 15:13–16 is an intrusion into Ea, separating the ceremony which is described in 15:9–12 and completed in 15:17,[30] and that 17:15–22 similarly interrupts 17:10–14, 17:23-27 which discusses the circumcision.[31] But it seems rather odd that this would have happened independently in both covenant accounts. The fact that 15:13–16 and 17:15–22 both contain a second divine communication to Abra(ha)m concerning his promised offspring militates against von Rad's contention. We should rather see in Ea and E′a a master at work who has gracefully produced, to use von Rad's words, "a unified structure and continuity."

The two covenant chapters are both followed by annunciation scenes, Eb and E′b. They continue the same order established in Ea and E′a.

- xi. Both episodes do not move directly to annunciation, rather 16:1–6 and 18:1–8 each set the scene for the pronouncement of conception and each is characterized by a high percentage of dialogue.
- xii. Only then do the actual annunciations follow, in 16:7–16 and 18:9–16.

Furthermore, two important theme-words appear in each section.

- xiii. The verbal root *šmᶜ*, 'hear,' in 16:11 is central to Eb; and it is important to E′b also, in 18:10.
- xiv. The annunciation in Eb closes with four uses of the root *rʾh*, 'see,' in 16:13–14; and this is echoed at the

[29] Von Rad, *Genesis*, 195.

[30] Von Rad, *Genesis*, 182; see also Skinner (*Genesis*, 282) who claims that these verses "are obviously out of place."

[31] Von Rad, *Genesis*, 197–98.

end of E'b with *yārēʾâ*, 'was afraid.' Although from different roots, these words, one dealing with Hagar and God and one dealing with Sarah and God, are assonant and accordingly link the stories.

Above it was noted that Isaac's birth in 21:1–7 in C'c is not parallel to Ishmael's birth in Cc. Obviously the corollary is also true. Ishmael's birth is recorded in 16:15–16 in Eb but if finds no corresponding announcement of Isaac's birth in E'b. The reason for this has already been stated: to the Hebrews, the births of the heroes were secondary to their annunciations. This is equally true of Ugaritic epic, where the events leading to the births of Danel's and Kret's children receive much more attention than the births themselves. Accordingly, in the Abraham Cycle the annunciations of Hagar and Sarah prompting the births of Ishmael and Isaac are parallel, but the births themselves are not.

THE TWO CONTROLS

The structure posited by Cassuto over thirty years ago has stood up to detailed examination. We can reaffirm his general conclusion that "all this shows clearly how out of the material selected from the store of ancient tradition concerning Abraham a homogeneous narrative was created in the text before us, integrated and harmoniously arranged in all its parts and details."[32] The general view that "the crude and disjointed tales of the Patriarchs" are unpolished and unsophisticated[33] is simply inaccurate. The compiler has artfully created a palistrophe[34] at which we can marvel. But we do not have to stop here.

[32] Cassuto, *From Noah to Abraham*, 297.

[33] See D. B. Redford, *A Study of the Biblical Story of Joseph* (Leiden, 1970) 1.

[34] This term seems to have been invented by McEvenue (*The Narrative Style of the Priestly Writer*, 29, n 18) and has since been borrowed by other writers. McEvenue describes it thus: "The figure is experienced as a thought which stretches outward over a certain series of elements

The redactor has set up his ten units—or with the subsections in C and C′ and E and E′ we may more properly speak of sixteen units—in more than just a chiastic parallelism. He introduced two new onomastic entries at the pivot point of the narrative. This pivot, at which the episodes of 11:27–16:16 are then repeated in reverse order in 17:1–22:24, is 17:1–5. Here all the important aspects of Abraham's life come together. He is 99 years old, his age at Sarah's conception of Isaac. God appears to him as El Shaddai, the distinctively patriarchal divine name (see Exod 6:3). Abraham walks with God at this point. And the covenant is established.

In the next verses we encounter two new names. Here Elohim is introduced for the first time. Up to this point, only Yahweh has been used (along with two El names in 14:20, 14:22, 16:13). Henceforth Yahweh will alternate with Elohim (along with one El name in 21:33). We gain the impression that Abraham's religious journey was not complete in 11:27–16:16. It is as if Hebrew theology is unfulfilled without Yahweh *and* Elohim, as *one* god. Moreover, just as the divine partner in the covenant gains a new name at this juncture, so does the human partner. Henceforth the patriarch will be known as Abraham. In A through E he is called Abram, in E′ through A′ he is Abraham.[35]

---

and then retraces its steps over the same elements. It can be merely a mannerism. But it can also be an effective figure if the repeated elements are key words, and if the thought continues to develop in such a way that a tension or contrast is felt between the first and second occurrence of each element, and between the ideas which are made to correspond in this way."

[35] This point has been reached quite independently by J. M. Sasson, "The Biographic Mode in Hebrew Historiography," in *In the Shelter of Elyon: Essays on Ancient Palestinian Life and Literature in Honor of G. W. Ahlström* (ed. W. B. Barrick and J. R. Spencer; Sheffield, 1984) 307: "This particular series of scenes is complicated by the fact that the collection is, for theological reasons, allocated to materials concerning Abram and to those concerning Abraham."

I refer to the two names introduced at the pivot point as controls, for they indicate that the redactional structuring posited for the Abraham Cycle is a well-pondered design. If one is not convinced by the large number of themes and theme-words common to the parallel story lines in the inverse sequences of 11:27–16:16 and 17:1–22:24, then these controls should dispel any doubt. The first of these controls, the use of the divine names Yahweh and Elohim, is unquestionably the central factor in Pentateuchal source criticism. Accordingly, any conclusions which might be drawn from the use of the two theophores in the Abraham Cycle relevant to source analysis, is a topic which will be taken up later in some detail (see below, chap. VI).

CATCHWORDS

In chap. I we saw that key vocabulary items are used in the Primeval History not only to link parallel units but to link successive units as well. This is also the case, indeed even more so, in the Abraham Cycle. This literary technique is so prevalent it is perhaps best to list these catchwords and phrases.

A is a very short unit but it nevertheless contains two items which anticipate B:

i. *môladt-*, 'homeland,' occurs in 11:28 and 12:1.
ii. *ʾarṣā kᵉnaʿan*, 'to the land of Canaan,' appears in 11:31 and 12:5 (bis).

Numerous catchwords and phrases link section B to section C:

i. *wᵉhakkᵉnaʿănî ʾaz bāʾāreṣ*, 'the Canaanite was then in the land,' occurs in 12:6; and *wᵉhakkᵉnaʿănî wᵉhappᵉrizzî ʾaz yôšēb bāʾāreṣ*, 'the Canaanite and Perizzite then dwelled in the land,' occurs in 13:7.
ii. The giving of the land *lᵉzarʿăkā*, 'to your seed,' occurs in 12:7 and 13:15.
iii. *miqqedem*, 'eastward,' occurs in 12:8 and 13:11.

iv. *wayyiben šām mizbēaḥ laYHWH*, 'he built there an altar to Yahweh,' occurs in 12:8 and 13:18.
v. Bethel and Ai are prominent in 12:8 and 13:3.[36]
vi. Abram calls *bᵉšēm YHWH*, 'on the name of Yahweh,' in 12:8 and 13:4.
vii. The roots *hlk* and *nsᶜ*, 'go' and 'travel,' are used in 12:9 and 13:2.
viii. *hannegbā*, 'to the Negev,' appears in 12:9 and 13:1.

Two nexuses bridge C and D:

i. *ṣōᶜar*, 'Zoar,' occurs in 13:10 and 14:2, 14:8.
ii. Lot's dwelling in Sodom appears in 13:12 and 14:12.

No two units in the Abraham Cycle are as dissimilar as D and E. In the former the patriarch is the military chieftain and in the latter he is the covenant partner of God. Nonetheless, as Sarna has pointed out,[37] the compiler used a number of words to link the episodes:

i. *miggēn*, 'delivered,' appears in 14:20, and *māgēn*, 'shield,' is used in 15:1.
ii. *rᵉkūš*, 'property, wealth, substance,' occurs in 14:21 and 15:14.
iii. Damascus is worked into the stories in 14:15 and 15:2.
iv. *bᵉrît*, 'alliance, covenant,' appears in 14:13 and 15:18.
v. *hâʾĕmôrî*, 'the Amorite,' occurs twice in each unit, in 14:7, 14:13, and 15:10, 15:21.

Other connections not mentioned by Sarna are as follows:

vi. *rᵉpāʾîm*, 'Rephaim,' occurs in 14:5 and 15:20.
vii. *dān*, 'Dan, judge,' appears in 14:14 and 15:14.
viii. *ṣedeq*, 'Zedek,' occurs in 14:18, and *ṣᵉdāqâ*, 'righteousness,' is used in 15:6.
ix. *šālēm*, 'Salem, complete,' is used in 14:18 and 15:16.

[36] This and the next three examples were noted by Cassuto, *From Noah to Abraham*, 364. Doubtless many more of these would have been mentioned by him had he lived to complete his commentary on Genesis.

[37] Sarna, *Understanding Genesis*, 121–22.

E and E′ are not only successive but parallel so they share many features, as shown in the discussion about their correspondence. But it is specifically the subsections Eb and E′a which are contiguous, so it is noteworthy that they too have catchwords and phrases linking them:

i. *ʾarbeh*, 'I will multiply,' is used in 16:10 and 17:2.
ii. The root *šmʿ*, 'hear,' is predicated of God in 16:11 and 17:20.
iii. Ishmael dominates 16:11–16 and appears in 17:20 too.
iv. We are given Abra(ha)m's age, obviously in similar wording, in 16:16 and 17:1.

E′ is linked to the following D′ through these nexuses:

i. *petaḥ*, 'entrance,' occurs in 18:1 as Abraham greets his visitors, and *happetḥâ*, 'at the entrance,' is used in 19:6 as Lot greets his visitors.
ii. The same root occurs in *niṣṣābîm*, 'standing,' in 18:2 and *nᵉṣîb*, 'pillar,' in 18:26.
iii. *wayyištaḥû* (*ʾappayim*) *ʾārṣâ*, 'he prostrated (his face) earthward,' appears in 18:2 and 19:1.
iv. Abraham's hospitality in 18:3–8 is echoed by Lot's hospitality in 19:2–3.
v. A paranomasia of sort is achieved by the roots *ṣḥq*, 'laugh,' in 18:12–15, and *ṣʿq/zʿq*, 'cry' in 18:20–21.

The following catchwords bridge D′ and C′:

i. *gôy gādôl*, 'a great nation,' appears in 18:18 and 21:18.
ii. *qûm qaḥ*, 'get up, take,' occurs in 19:15, and *qûmî śᵉʾî*, 'get up, take,' occurs in 21:18.
iii. The Hiphʿil of *ḥzq*, 'seize, take hold,' is used in 19:16 and 21:18.
iv. The Hiphʿil of *šqh*, 'give drink,' is used in 19:32–35 and 21:19.
v. The root *hrh*, 'conceive,' occurs in 19:36 and 21:2.

Two nexuses link C′ and B′:

i. *wayyiqqaḥ ʾabrāhām*, 'Abraham took,' appears in 21:27 and 22:6.
ii. Beersheba occurs in 21:33 and 22:19.

Finally, even A′, the most loosely connected unit of the Abraham Cycle, has a link with the preceding B′, as noted by Jacob:[38]

i. *wayᵉhî ʾaḥar/ʾaḥărê haddᵉbārîm hāʾēlleh,* 'after these things,' commences both units, in 22:1 and 22:20.

This large number of catchwords has been utilized by the redactor to further correlate the stories which comprise the Abraham Cycle into a unified whole. Any one of these examples could be a coincidence, this is true. But taken collectively, the cumulative weight of the data permits us to conclude that we have here a deliberate attempt by an ancient Israelite genius to tighten the web he has woven.

THE END OF THE ABRAHAM CYCLE

In the schema proposed by Cassuto and adopted herein with some modifications, the Abraham Cycle ends with chap. 22.[39] Obviously there is more material about the patriarch's life, but it is not central to his spiritual odyssey. As Sarna has written, "With the climax of his career now behind him, Abraham's subsequent acts are concerned with winding up his affairs."[40] This material, which comprises 23:1–25:18, may be divided into five units: A. Death and burial of Sarah (23:1–20), B. Marriage of Isaac (24:1–67), C. Abraham's sons (25:1–6), D. Death and burial of Abraham (25:7–11), E. Ishmael's sons (25:12–18).

If one looks at the entire redactional process of Genesis, one realizes that these units do not constitute a cycle unto itself. Rather, they are used to link the second major

[38] Jacob, *Das erste Buch der Tora: Genesis,* 504.

[39] This view is expressed by others as well. Von Rad, *Genesis,* 241, states: "The narrative about Abraham's sacrifice was the climax . . . and the end of the Abraham narratives." Davidson (*Genesis 12–50,* 98) states: "This narrative (chapter 22) marks the end of Abraham's spiritual experience."

[40] Sarna, *Understanding Genesis,* 166.

cycle of the book, that of Abraham, with the third cycle, that of Jacob.[41] Moreover, as we shall see in chap. IV, these units are paralleled by the material which connects the Jacob Cycle with the last portion of Genesis, the Joseph Cycle. Accordingly, a detailed analysis of 23:1–25:18 will be discussed later.

It is noteworthy that 23:1–25:18 is exactly the same as Parshat Ḥayye Sarah in the rabbinic division of the Torah for the Jewish annual reading cycle. In other words, the rabbis sensed that these units were not primary to the life of Abraham which they saw as the portions Lek Leka and Wayyera. In chap. I we saw that the pivot point of the Primeval Cycle accords with the rabbinic division of Genesis into the portions Bereshit and Noaḥ Consequently, we can conclude that behind the traditional Jewish apportionment of the text is a thought process not too inconsistent with the findings of modern biblical scholarship. Of course, we would not want to carry this argument too far. Whereas Parshat Noaḥ ends at 11:32, I see the Primeval History ending at 11:26 (only a slight difference); and though Lek Leka and Wayyera divide the Abraham Cycle at 18:1, I see the pivot point at 17:1 (a more significant difference).[42]

OVERVIEW

In the past most scholars have viewed the Abraham narratives as a loose collection of stories brought together in a more or less haphazard or ad hoc fashion. Cassuto

[41] Concerning chap. 24, for example, Morgenstern (*The Book of Genesis*, 191) writes: "The story of Isaac's obtaining his cousin Rebekah, artistic and spiritual though it is, is nevertheless in itself an independent incident of the Abraham cycle of stories, without which the unity of the Abraham story would nevertheless have been complete. It is merely the connecting link between the Abraham cycle and the Jacob cycle. . . ."

[42] In the triennial reading cycle, there are much shorter pericopes and thus we will expect even more accord with the plan laid out in this book. The triennial system adduced by A. Buechler and others is

proposed a chiastic parallelism for the episodes in 12:1–22:19. Since this material is bounded by two genealogical bookends, I have expanded the Abraham Cycle to include all of 11:27-22:24. Within these chapters we may note 1) five units in 11:27–16:16 which are then duplicated by five units in reverse order in 17:1–22:24; 2) a large series of theme-words and parallel expressions and ideas which link the matching units; 3) the focal point of the Abraham Cycle at 17:1–5; 4) two controls, the introduction of the divine element Elohim and the patriarch's name change from Abram to Abraham, which point to the correctness of our proposed structure; and 5) catchwords and phrases which link successive units. The presence of these devices in the narrative betokens a well-conceived blueprint expertly executed by the individual responsible for bringing together the various traditions surrounding Israel's first patriarch. In keeping with the terminology adopted in this book, we may label this the redactional structuring of the Abraham Cycle.

---

conveniently presented in *Encyclopaedia Judaica* 15 (1971) cols. 1387–88. There it is noted that a division occurs at 17:1, our focal point in the Abraham Cycle.

III

THE JACOB CYCLE

The stories which commence with Jacob's birth in 25:19–26 and conclude with Benjamin's birth in 35:16–22 are generally recognized to be an integrated narrative complex.[1] In 1975, Michael Fishbane advanced our understanding of these chapters by demonstrating most conclusively that the stories of the Jacob Cycle are aligned in perfectly symmetrical fashion.[2] In other words, redactional structuring may be detected not only in the Primeval History and the Abraham Cycle but in the third major division of Genesis as well. The structure of the Jacob Cycle as outlined below is essentially that of Fishbane's, though I have made one slight adjustment.[3]

- A Oracle sought, struggle in childbirth, Jacob born (25:19–34)
- B Interlude: Rebekah in foreign palace, pact with foreigners (26:1–34)
- C Jacob fears Esau and flees (27:1–28:9)
- D Messengers (28:10–22)
- E Arrival at Haran (29:1–30)

[1] G. von Rad, *Genesis* (Philadelphia, 1961) 258; and J. Morgenstern, *The Book of Genesis* (New York, 1965) 184–205.

[2] M. Fishbane, "Composition and Structure in the Jacob Cycle (Gen. 25:19–35:22)," *JJS* 26 (1975) 15–38. A slightly altered version of this article appears as chap. 3 in M. Fishbane, *Text and Texture* (New York, 1979) 40–62.

[3] What Fishbane calls F, I divide into F and F′. In "Composition and Structure," 32, and *Text and Texture*, 56–57, he recognizes that two units are present but does not label them as such. Also, Fishbane considers 29:31–35 part of E whereas I attach it to F.

F Jacob's wives are fertile (29:31–30:24)
F′ Jacob's flocks are fertile (30:25–43)
E′ Flight from Haran (31:1–54)
D′ Messengers (32:1–32)
C′ Jacob returns and fears Esau (33:1–20)
B′ Interlude: Dinah in foreign palace, pact with foreigners (34:1–31)
A′ Oracle fulfilled, struggle in childbirth, Jacob becomes Israel (35:1–22)

A detailed investigation of the Jacob Cycle has been executed expertly by Fishbane, so that what follows is in large part merely a rewording or reorganization of his work. Before proceeding to an analysis of each of the paired units in 25:19–35:22, let me take this opportunity to gratefully acknowledge Professor Fishbane's permission to reproduce freely in my own words the findings of his excellent studies.[4]

A ORACLE SOUGHT, STRUGGLE IN CHILDBIRTH, JACOB BORN (25:19–34)

A′ ORACLE FULFILLED, STRUGGLE IN CHILDBIRTH, JACOB BECOMES ISRAEL (35:1–22)

As is well known, the Jacob Cycle is fraught with tensions and conflicts. Fishbane noted that these various themes—fraternal strife, deception, barrenness, etc.—all appear in 25:19–34 in proleptic form and do not entirely disappear until the Cycle's denouement in 35:1–22. He backs up this proposition with a number of items which cement the relationship between A and A′.

i. An oracle is sought in 25:23 which predicts the ascendancy of Jacob. The oracle is fulfilled in 35:11–12 with

[4] In the interest of economy, I refrain from citing the page numbers of each of the points raised by Fishbane. The interested reader is requested to consult the two works listed in n 2 above, both of which are easily available.

God telling Jacob the full extent of the greatness in store for him.[5]

ii. Rebekah struggles in childbirth in 25:21–22; and Rachel suffers far worse in her delivery in 35:16–20.

iii. Jacob is born and named in 25:26. Jacob's name is changed to Israel in 35:10.[6]

iv. Central to A is the *bᵉkôrâ*, 'birthright,' in 25:31–34; and central to A′ is the *bᵉrākâ*, 'blessing,' in 35:9–12, as indicated by *wayᵉbārek*, 'he (God) blessed,' in 35:9.

Still other features and theme-words serve to unite the first and last units of the Jacob Cycle.

v. Parental differences are noted in 25:28 where Isaac favors Esau and Rebekah favors Jacob. Parental differences reoccur in 35:18 where Rachel gives her son a pejorative name, Ben-oni, while Jacob gives him a propitious name, Benjamin.

vi. The first hint at fraternal strife appears in 25:29–34, and the Jacob–Esau struggle is last mentioned in 35:1, 35:7.

vii. In 25:23 we read how primogeniture will be set aside among Isaac's sons. In 35:22 we learn the circumstances which will lead to the abrogation of this rule among Jacob's sons.

viii. *mippaddan ʾărām*, 'from Paddan Aram,' obtains in 25:20 and 35:9.

ix. The root *rbh* occurs in 25:23 with *rab*, 'older,' and in 35:11 with *rᵉbēh*, 'multiply.'

x. The root *gdl* occurs in 25:27 with *wayyigdᵉlû*, 'they (the boys) grew,' and in 35:21 with *migdal*, 'Migdal.'

[5] God has blessed Jacob similarly earlier in the Cycle, but this is by far the most complete and important of the speeches. The wording is very reminiscent of God's talk to Abraham in 17:6, 17:8, the focal point of all divine communications to the first patriarch. See further von Rad, *Genesis*, 334.

[6] Of course he properly receives the new name in 32:29, but he is not referred to in the narratives as Israel until after 35:10, e.g., in 35:21–22. Earlier references to Israel may be interpreted as references to the nation; for 32:33 this is obvious and on 33:20, see J. Skinner, *Genesis* (New York, 1910) 416.

xi. In 25:27 we read of Jacob *yôšēb ʾōhālîm*, 'a dweller in tents'; and in 35:21 we read about the patriarch *wayyēṭ ʾōhŏlōh*, 'he pitched his tent.'

xii. We are not told specifically that Rebekah received any assistance in childbirth and childrearing in 25:21–26, but we might assume that Deborah was present. In 35:8 we read of Deborah's death and she is specifically called *mêneqet ribqâ*, 'Rebekah's wet-nurse.'

As in the previous chapters, we are able to gain an understanding of the compiler's modus operandi by paying attention to redactional structuring. A is a very unified story with each of its smaller episodes leading neatly from one to the other. Isaac's marriage to Rebekah, Rebekah's sterility and Isaac's entreaty, Rebekah's childbearing, the boys' growing up, and the introductory fraternal strife all flow very naturally. A′, on the other hand, is very clearly "a series of fragmentary excerpts"[7] which do not naturally interconnect. But each of these fragments at the close of the Cycle has a clear purpose: to evoke in the reader's mind the start of the Cycle. 35:1–7 recalls the strife with Esau now finally over, 35:8 suggests the boys' births, 35:9–15 brings to mind Jacob's naming, the oracle delivered to Rebekah, and the *bᵉkôrâ/bᵉrākâ* relation, 35:16–20 prompts the struggle in Rebekah's womb, and 35:21–22 raises the issue of the firstborn's fall from favor. Accordingly, the redactor has utilized most economically the short pieces brought together in 35:1–22 to link this unit with the single episode in 25:19–34.

B INTERLUDE: REBEKAH IN FOREIGN PALACE, PACT WITH FOREIGNERS (26:1–34)

B′ INTERLUDE: DINAH IN FOREIGN PALACE, PACT WITH FOREIGNERS (34:1–31)

It does not take more than a brief look at these two units to conclude that they are anomalous within the

[7] Skinner, *Genesis*, 422.

Jacob Cycle. Individual commentators have realized this before,[8] but Genesis scholarship had to wait for Fishbane's work on the structure of the Cycle to learn that this was done purposely. That is to say, within the Cycle of stories concerning the third patriarch, by design the second and next-to-last episodes have no direct connection with the narrative at large. Fishbane writes:

> . . . we first note that *both* chapters are anomalous in their context and that both are in symmetrical relationship to each other. To move from an observational to a functional-evaluative standpoint the issue can be stated differently: Gen. 26 serves as a narrative interlude between the opening tensions and their historical development; similarly, Gen. 34 serves as an interlude between the reconciliation between Jacob and Esau and the final resolution and blessing at Beth-El.[9]

Fishbane recognized the following common features and theme-words in B and B′.

i. As implied in the above quotation, B has no connection with A immediately preceding it or C immediately following it. The same is true of B′ vis-à-vis C′ and A′.
ii. As also implied above, B "increases the tension of the developing action" whereas B′ "delays the denouement and release of the entire Cycle."[10]
iii. B concerns the early Israelite interaction with the Philistines, the uncircumcised people par excellence in the Bible (though *ᶜārēl/ᶜărēlîm*, 'uncircumcised,' is not specifically used in this chapter). B′ concerns the early Israelite interaction with the uncircumcised Shechemites; cf. *ᶜorlâ*, 'foreskin,' in 34:14.
iv. Isaac deceives Abimelech in 26:7 and Jacob's sons deceive the Shechemites in 34:13–29.

[8] On 26:1–34 see, for example, Skinner (*Genesis*, 355) who terms it "misplaced"; on 34:1–31 see, among others, E. A. Speiser (*Genesis* [Garden City, NY, 1964] 266) who says, "The narrative is unusual on more counts than one."

[9] Fishbane, "Composition and Structure," 24.

[10] Fishbane, "Composition and Structure," 24.

v. A pact is formed between Isaac and Abimelech in 26:26–33 and a treaty between Jacob's family and Schechem is proposed in 34:8–23.

vi. *ʾăḥôt-*, 'sister,' is used in 26:7, 26:9, and in 34:13, 34:14.

vii. The verbal root *škb*, 'lie,' occurs in 26:10 and in 34:2, 34:7.

viii. *ʾāḥîw*, 'his brother,' appears in 26:31; and *ʾaḥehā*, 'her brothers,' appears in 34:11.

Beyond these similarities pointed out by Fishbane may be noted one important theme and numerous theme-words.

ix. Rebekah in Abimelech's palace and Dinah in Shechem's palace are reflexes of the common East Mediterranean "Helen of Troy" motif.[11]

x. The Hiphʿil of *rbh* occurs in 26:4 with *wᵉhirbêtî*, 'I will multiply,' and in 34:12 with *harbû*, 'increase.'

xi. The verbal root *hrg*, 'kill,' is used in 26:7 and 34:25–26.

xii. In 26:10 we have the expression *ʾaḥad hāʿām*, 'one of the people'; and in 34:22 we have *ʿam ʾeḥād*, 'one people.'

xiii. *miqnēh*, 'flock,' appears in 26:14 (bis); and the same word with pronominal suffixes is used in 34:5, 34:23.

xiv. The root *rḥb* is used to denote expanse of land and ample room in which two parties may coexist in 26:22 with *rᵉḥôbôt*, 'Rehoboth,' and *hirḥîb*, 'expanded,' and in 34:21 with *raḥăbat*, 'expanse.'

xv. Abimelech's cohort in 26:26 is named *ʾăḥuzzat*, 'Ahuzzath'; and the same root obtains in *hēʾāḥăzû*, 'acquire real estate,' in 34:10.

xvi. Of different roots and different meanings but very alike in sound are *bênôtênû*, 'between us,' in 26:28, and *bᵉnôtênû*, 'our daughters,' in 34:9, 34:21.

xvii. A key word in 26:29, 26:31 is *šālôm*, 'peace'; and the same root is used in 34:21 with *šᵉlēmîm*, 'friendly, upright.'

In short, these two pericopes have little or nothing to do with the Jacob Cycle storyline and appear to have little in

[11] See further C. H. Gordon, *The Common Background of Greek and Hebrew Civilizations* (New York, 1965) 285.

common with each other. But deeper investigation has turned up several similar motifs in B and B′ and numerous theme-words which link them together. Furthermore, they function in the same way within the Cycle, as important interludes craftly placed by our master compiler.

C JACOB FEARS ESAU AND FLEES (27:1–28:9)

C′ JACOB RETURNS AND FEARS ESAU (33:1–20)

After the interlude of 26:1–34, the story returns to developing the tension between Jacob and Esau first suggested in 25:19–34. Before the interlude of 34:1–31, that same tension appears as Jacob and Esau reunite after years apart. Fishbane noted the following similarities between C and C′.

i. Jacob deceives Isaac in 27:18–29 and Jacob plans to deceive Esau in 33:1–2.
ii. Jacob fears Esau in 27:41–45 and again in 33:1–8.
iii. Jacob flees Canaan in 28:5 and he returns to Canaan in 33:18.
iv. Perhaps most important of all, Jacob steals the *b^erākâ*, 'blessing,' from Esau in 27:18–29, but returns it to him in 33:11.
v. The verbal root *nšq*, 'kiss,' occurs in 27:26–27 and in 33:4.

These are, of course, the most important features shared by the two episodes and they are enough to ascertain the relationship between them. But there are many more theme-words which can be cited which serve to further link 27:1–28:9 and 33:1–20.

vi. C begins *wattikhenā ᶜênāw mêrᵉ˒ôt*, literally 'his (Isaac's) eyes had faded from seeing,' after which Esau enters the scene. C′ begins *wayiśśā˒ yaᶜăqōb ᶜênāw wayyar˒*, 'Jacob lifted his eyes and saw,' after which Esau again enters the picture.
vii. Jacob brings (Hiphᶜil of *bw˒*) good things to Isaac in 27:10, 27:14; and he brings (Hophᶜal of *bw˒*) good things to Esau in 33:11.

viii. The verbal root *ngš*, 'approach, come near, bring near,' is used in 27:21–22, 27:25–27, and in 33:6–7.

ix. The pun on the root *śʿr* used whenever Esau is spoken of is achieved here as well. In 27:23 we read *śᵉʿîrôt*, 'hairy'; and in 33:14, 33:16 we have *śēʿîrâ*, 'to Seir.'

x. Irony is introduced into the stories. In 27:28 we read that Jacob will receive *rôb*, 'abundance'; but in 33:9 it is Esau who appears as *rāb*, 'abundant.'

xi. Further irony occurs in 27:29 with *wᵉyištaḥăwû*, 'will bow down,' and in 33:3 with *wayyištaḥû*, 'bowed down.' In the first instance it is Jacob's brothers who are to pay homage to him, but in the second case it is Jacob prostrating himself to Esau!

xii. Similarly, in 27:40 Esau is told he will throw off the yoke *mēʿal ṣawwāʾrekā*, 'from your neck'; and in 33:4 we read *wayyippōl ʿal ṣawwāʾrāw*, 'he (Esau) fell on his (Jacob's) neck.' The brothers' necks also converge at 27:16 where Jacob uses goatskins to disguise the smoothness of his neck in imitation of Esau's neck.

xiii. Irony is also achieved by the use of the consonants *pʿmym*. In 27:36 Esau bemoans that Jacob has tricked him *paʿămayim*, 'two times'; but in the end it is Jacob who prostrates himself before Esau *šebaʿ pᵉʿāmîm*, 'seven times,' in 33:3.

xiv. *wayyēbk*, 'he (Esau) cried,' appears in 27:38; and *wayyibkû*, 'they (Esau and Jacob) cried,' occurs in 33:4. If we accept the suggestion of some textual critics to emend *wayyibkû* to *wayyēbk* in 33:4 due to haplography (the next word begins with *waw*),[12] then the likeness is exact; in each case we would understand that Esau alone cried.

xv. Not only are the stories the flight from and return to Canaan (see point iii above), but conversely they are the flight to and return from Paddan Aram, mentioned specifically in 28:2–7 and 33:18.

xvi. Esau learns of Jacob's marriage plans in 28:6–7, then meets the wives in 33:5–7.

xvii. Perhaps the greatest irony of all, in each vignette in C there are always only two individuals present but never

[12] Skinner, *Genesis* 413; Speiser, *Genesis*, 259; and *BHS*, ad loc.

Jacob and Esau together.[13] In C′, when the conflict is at last settled, it is the two brothers who hug and kiss and engage each other in long conversation.

These seventeen points show conclusively that C and C′ are matching episodes. Recognition of this fact will again allow us to understand a literary critical problem which has long been debated by Genesis commentators. Scholars have noted that the Jacob stories can be separated into a group of Transjordanian ones and a group of Cisjordanian ones.[14] Whatever the value of this division, it is clear that C′ traces Jacob's reentry into Canaan either through Succoth (33:17) or through Shechem (33:18). While it is true that the two can be reconciled geographically,[15] it nevertheless seems that we have variant traditions concerning the patriarch's itinerary.

But since C and C′ are paired units, we are able to determine why there are two traditions at this juncture. There need to be two reentry sites because 27:1–28:9 records for us two reasons for fleeing in the first place. On the one hand we have Esau's anger as a cause for leaving, and on the other hand we have Isaac's and Rebekah's mutual desire for Jacob not to marry a Canaanite.[16] And while it is true that these two ideas can also be reconciled, for the text as we have it is certainly coherent,[17] there are nevertheless two motives for leaving. In other words, as a finished product—regardless of the prehistory of the narratives—the Jacob Cycle is symmetrical

[13] This was noted by B. Jacob (*Das erste Buch der Tora: Genesis* [Berlin, 1934] 577) but to my knowledge no other commentator has pointed this out.

[14] R. de Vaux, *The Early History of Israel* (Philadelphia, 1978) 172–73.

[15] Y. Aharoni and M. Avi-Yonah, *The Macmillan Bible Atlas* (New York, 1977) 29, map 27.

[16] See von Rad, *Genesis*, 276; S. R. Driver, *The Book of Genesis* (London, 1906) 262; Speiser, *Genesis*, 215–16; Morgenstern, *The Book of Genesis*, 223; and R. Davidson, *Genesis 12–50* (Cambridge, 1979) 142–43.

[17] See D. Kidner, *Genesis* (Downers Grove, IL, 1967) 157; Fishbane, "Composition and Structure," 26; and Fishbane, *Text and Texture*, 48–49.

even within its symmetry. Not only are the stories of Jacob's leaving and homecoming matched, but there are two reasons for parting from Canaan and thus two routes for returning to Canaan.

D MESSENGERS (28:10–22)

D′ MESSENGERS (32:1–32)

Fishbane notes that between Jacob's leaving Canaan in C and his arriving in Haran in E there occurs the episode which has the patriarch encountering divine messengers. Symmetrical with this is a unit of several stories concerning messengers, both human and divine, sandwiched between Jacob's leaving Haran in E′ and his return to Canaan in C′.[18] Fishbane noted the following parallels between 28:10–22 and 32:1–32.

i. D begins with a reference to Jacob's journey to Haran in 28:10; and D′ begins with the final parting of Jacob and Laban in 32:1.

ii. *malʾăkê ʾĕlôhîm*, 'messengers of God,' occurs in 28:12; and in the three sections comprising C′ we have *malʾăkê ʾĕlôhîm*, 'messengers of God,' in 32:2, *malʾākîm*, '(human) messengers,' in 32:4, 32:7, and *ʾĕlôhîm*, 'God,' in 32:31.

iii. The verbal root *pgʿ*, 'encounter,' is used in 28:11 and 32:2.

iv. Jacob receives a blessing in each unit and the root *brk*, 'bless,' is used specifically in 28:14 and 32:27, 32:30.

Again there are many more theme-words and ideas shared by the two units.

v. *māqôm*, 'place,' is ubiquitous in 28:11–19, and *mᵉqōmô*, 'his place,' occurs in 32:1.

vi. *wayyālen šām*, 'he spent the night there,' appears in 28:11 and 32:14, each time referring to Jacob.

vii. In 28:13 we read *ʾĕlōhê ʾabrāhām ʾabîkā wêʾlōhê yiṣḥāq*, 'the God of Abraham your father and the God of Isaac';

[18] Parts of what follow were also noted by Davidson (*Genesis 12–50*, 179) and von Rad (*Genesis*, 310–11).

and in 32:10 we have *ʾĕlōhê ʾābî ʾabrāhām wêʾlōhê ʾābî yiṣḥāq*, 'the God of my father Abraham and the God of my father Isaac.' In each case the pronouns refer to Jacob and in each case there is an identification with Yahweh.

viii. *zarʿekā/zarʿăkā*, 'your seed,' occurs in 28:13 and in 32:13.

ix. The verbal root *šwb*, 'return,' referring to returning to the land of Canaan, obtains in 28:15 and 32:10.[19]

x. *wayyîrāʾ*, 'was awed/afraid,' is predicated of Jacob in 28:17 and 32:8.

xi. *wayyaškēm yaʿăqōb babbôqer*, 'Jacob arose in the morning,' is used in 28:18; and *wayyaškēm lābān babbōqer*, 'Laban arose in the morning,' is used in 32:1.

xii. In 28:19 we read *wayyiqrāʾ ʾet šēm hammaqôm hahûʾ*, 'he (Jacob) called the name of that place'; and in 32:3 we have *wayyiqrāʾ šem hammaqôm hahûʾ*, 'he (Jacob) called the name of that place,' and in 32:31 we have *wayyiqrāʾ yaʿăqōb šēm hammaqôm*, 'Jacob called the name of the place.'

xiii. The encounter at Bethel ends with Jacob's recognition of the divine aspect of the event in 28:17; and the encounter at Peniel ends with the patriarch's recognition of the divine character of that event in 32:31.

xiv. After each encounter there is reference to a particular Israelite custom; in 28:22 it is tithing and in 32:33 it is the refrain from eating the hip sinew.

The stories in these units are among the oddest and most difficult to interpret in the Bible. That they purposely parallel each other has been demonstrated by Fishbane and reaffirmed here.

E ARRIVAL AT HARAN (29:1–30)
E′ FLIGHT FROM HARAN (31:1–54)

Units E, F, F′, and E′ form what Fishbane calls "the inner tale," that is, the story of Jacob and Laban within

[19] This point and the two preceding ones, and the general tenor of 28:13–15 and 32:10–13, were also recognized by Davidson (*Genesis 12–50*, 183).

the greater span of the Jacob Cycle. As the Cycle as a whole reflects redactional structuring, so does the inner tale where symmetry may also be observed. E relates Jacob's arrival at Haran and his meeting and negotiations with Laban. E′ relates Jacob's departure from Haran and his parting from and final negotiations with Laban. Fishbane pointed out these similarities between the two episodes.

i. The verbal root *nšq*, 'kiss,' directs our attention to Jacob's kissing Rachel in 29:11 and Laban's kissing Jacob in 29:13 during the arrival scene, and then to Laban's complaint in 31:28 that he was unable even to kiss his children goodbye before they left.
ii. Laban recognizes his oneness with Jacob with *ʿaṣmî ûbśārî ʾāttâ*, 'you are my bone and my flesh,' in 29:14; and then says *nikrᵉtâ bᵉrît ʾănî wāʾāttâ*, 'let us make a pact, you and I,' in 31:44.
iii. Central to the discussion in each chapter is *maśkurt-*, '(Jacob's) wages,' in 29:15 and in 31:7, 31:41.
iv. The pacts are both marked by ceremonial meals, in 29:22 and in 31:46, 31:54.
v. Deception plays a role in each story, with Laban duping Jacob in 29:23–26 and in turn being deceived first by Jacob in 31:20 and then by Rachel in 31:33–35.

A few other shared theme-words further illuminate the bond between E and E′.

vi. *wᵉgālᵉlû ʾet hāʾeben*, 'to roll the stone,' in 29:3, 29:8, and *wayyāgel*, '(Jacob) rolled,' in 29:10, are echoed in 31:46 where *gāl*, 'mound,' and *ʾăbānîm*, 'stones,' are collocated.
vii. Shepherding plays a role in 29:1–10 and in 31:4–12, 31:38–39.
viii. Jacob refers to the general populus as *ʾaḥay*, 'my brothers,' in 29:4, and to his and Laban's families at large as *ʾaḥênû*, 'our brothers,' in 31:32.
ix. When deceived by Laban, Jacob responds *mah zzôʾt ʿāśîtā llî*, 'what is this you have done to me,' in 29:25; when the tables are turned, Laban says to Jacob *meh ʿāśîtā*, 'what have you done,' in 31:26.
x. Seven years and seven years are detailed in 29:20–30, and the same fourteen years are referred to in 31:41.

Clearly these two units are conceived as a matching pair, opening and closing the inner tale and forming the encasement for Jacob's success story at the center of the entire Cycle.

F JACOB'S WIVES ARE FERTILE (29:31–30:24)
F′ JACOB'S FLOCKS ARE FERTILE (30:25–43)

These two units stand at the center of the action and include within them the focus of the entire Cycle, as Fishbane correctly recognized. He pointed to the one major similarity between them and one common theme-word.

i. The main thrust of F is to detail the fertility of Jacob's wives and the main thrust of F′ is to describe the fertility of his flocks.
ii. *śᵉkārî*, 'my reward/payment,' is used in 30:18 and in 30:32–33 (see also 30:28).

But other similarities may also be noted.

iii. The root *yld*, 'bear,' occurs throughout 29:32–30:23 and is used in 30:39 also.
iv. Popular devices to increase fertility are used in each episode: the mandrakes in 30:14–16 and the wooden rods in 30:37–43.
v. Wordplays dominate F and a pun is incorporated into F′ with *lābān*, 'white,' and *libneh*, 'poplar,' in 30:35–37, amid numerous references to *lābān*, 'Laban.'[20]
vi. Perhaps another word play is intended by the names *rāḥēl*, 'Rachel,' and *lēʾâ*, 'Leah.' The former means 'ewe' and the latter may be etymologized as '(wild) cow.'[21] The reproduction of these female "animals" is echoed by the fertility of Jacob's real animals.

Throughout most of the Jacob Cycle things do not go too well for the patriarch. He strives with and fears

[20] See Davidson, *Genesis 12–50*, 166; Speiser, *Genesis*, 237; and von Rad, *Genesis*, 297.

[21] Skinner, *Genesis*, 383; Jacob, *Das erste Buch der Tora: Genesis*, 589; and BDB, 521.

his brother, he encounters and struggles with divine messengers, and he is duped by and then dictated to by his father-in-law. Even 34:1–31 which is not directly connected to the other narratives ends with Jacob in trouble. But F and F′, coming at the middle of the Cycle, are Jacob's successes and thus perfectly matched and meant for each other.

OVERVIEW

The Jacob Cycle reflects a deliberate structure in which the compiler has organized twelve individual units into reverse sequences. It is therefore akin to the palistrophe noticed for the Abraham Cycle. Fishbane first recognized the symmetry of the Jacob Cycle, and further investigation has shown his schema to be absolutely correct.

We are introduced to the Jacob narratives in A, then comes an interlude in B, and next follow Jacob's fear of Esau and his departure from Canaan in C, his encounter with messengers in D, his arrival at Haran in E, and his success through the fertility of his wives in F. At this juncture comes the focal point, to wit, 30:22–25 which bridges F and F′. The favored wife, Rachel, at long last gives birth, to the son who will eventually be the patriarch's favorite, Joseph. F′ begins with the telling statement, "After Rachel gave birth to Joseph, Jacob said to Laban, 'Give me leave that I may return to my homeland.'" Jacob has been successful throughout F, but the ultimate success is not realized until Rachel herself produces a son in 30:22–24. The very next verse, 30:25 translated above, connects this fact with Jacob's desire to return home.

Fishbane calls this "the archetechtonic pivot of the Cycle,"[22] the focus upon which all the action hinges. After this point all the themes and episodes of A through F are repeated in reverse order. In F′ we read of Jacob's success through the fertility of his flocks, then comes his flight

[22] Fishbane, "Composition and Structure," 32.

from Haran in E′, his encounters with messengers in D′, and the resolution of his fear of Esau and his return to Canaan in C′, next occurs an interlude in B′, and finally we have the denouement of the whole narrative in A′. The Jacob Cycle is unquestionably a masterpiece, well-conceived, brilliantly constructed, and expertly executed.

But the redactor did not stop here. As in the Primeval History and in the Abraham Cycle, incorporated into the Jacob Cycle are a series of nexuses linking successive units. The root *šbᶜ*, 'swear,' is used in A at 25:33 and in B at 26:32–34. Esau's marriages and the concern they caused his parents are the subject of a brief notice at the end of B at 26:34–35; this issue is echoed in C at 27:46–28:9. In C Jacob receives a blessing from his father at 27:27–29; and in D he gains God's blessing at 28:13–15. D and E share the word *ᵓeben*, 'stone,' in 28:18 and 29:10, with Jacob utilizing it in each instance. In E Jacob gains his two wives and their maid-servants in 29:23–30, and these four produce his children in F in 29:31–30:24.

F and F′ have a number of nexuses because they are not only successive but also paired in the redactional structure. Moreover, we may point to the focal point where 30:22–24 and 30:25 both mention Rachel's giving birth to Joseph in F and F′ respectively. F′ and E′ have in common the discussion of the flocks and their peculiar characteristics in 30:32–43 and in 31:8–12. The verbal root *nšq*, 'kiss,' in 31:28 and 32:1 bridges E′ and D′. Jacob's fear of Esau and attempted bribery appear in D′ at 32:4–22 and in C′ at 33:5–11. C′ ends with a reference to Shechem and Hamor in 33:19, a point which is loudly echoed throughout B′ in 34:1–27. The *benê yaᶜăqōb*, 'sons of Jacob,' and their exploits are prominent throughout B′ in 34:7–31; and they occur again in A′ at 35:5.

As with the first two major cycles of Genesis, the third one uses common ideas and vocabulary items to tie its various units into a neat bundle. Theme-words cement the relationship between parallel episodes, and catch-words tie each unit to the succeeding unit. These catch-words are especially important between A and B, B and C, C′ and B′, and B′ and A′, because they bring the two interludes, with no immediate connection to the Jacob narratives, into the mainstream of the Cycle. A notice such as 26:34–35 concerning Esau's wives and a reference to Shechem and Hamor at 33:19 are seemingly out of place, but they are important bridges between the interludes and the story at large.

In chaps. I and II we saw that the natural breaks in the structures of the Primeval History and the Abraham Cycle are often in agreement with the rabbinic division of Genesis. Therefore, it is apropos to comment on any accord between sections of the Jacob Cycle according to our analysis and according to the rabbis. It may be noted that 25:19 marks not only the beginning of the Jacob Cycle but also that of Parshat Toledot. Fishbane notes that the rabbinic division also attempts to isolate the inner tale, i.e., the Paddan Aram material along with the messenger encounters before and after it. Thus Parshat Wayyetze commences at 28:10 as does D, though we would extend it beyond 32:3 to include all of D′ which ends at 32:33.[23] Beyond this one can note, as does Fishbane, "that our thematic sub-divisions agree, almost completely, both with the chapter divisions introduced by Christian scholars in the Middle Ages and with the Massoretic unit divisions found in Rabbinic Bibles."[24] Of course, we end the Jacob Cycle at 35:22 whereas the third traditional Jewish portion in these chapters, Parshat Wayyishlaḥ concludes at 36:43. The extra material, obviously too short to comprise its own rabbinic division, is parallel to the material in Parshat Ḥayye Sarah (23:1–25:18) and will be discussed in the next chapter.

We can conclude this chapter by summarizing. The Jacob's story's unity has been recognized often in the past, but it took until 1975 for Fishbane to point out exactly how united the Cycle is. Deeper analysis confirms his conclusion. The redactor of these chapters 1) aligned the units in matching sequences of reverse

[23] Fishbane, "Composition and Structure," 30, n 43.
[24] Fishbane, "Composition and Structure," 21.

order, 2) included shared themes and theme-words in the parallel units, 3) hinged the Cycle on the pivot at 30:22–25, and 4) used nexuses to connect each successive unit.[25]

[25] For still other stylistic devices in the Jacob Cycle, see the detailed treatment by J. P. Fokkelman (*Narrative Art in Genesis* [Assen and Amsterdam, 1975] 83–241).

IV

THE LINKING MATERIAL

Genesis commentators have noted, quite accurately, that the patriarchal narratives can be divided into three sections, the Abraham Cycle, the Jacob Cycle, and the Joseph Cycle. Separating the three are two groups of material, the one serving to link the Abraham and Jacob Cycles, the other serving to link the Jacob and Joseph Cycles. These sections, 23:1–25:18 and 35:23–36:43, are hodgepodges of material which have been culled from various sources. But even here our compiler was able to evince a redactional structuring. Just as each cycle consists of matching sequences, so these two sections are conceived along parallel lines. None of the beauty of the longer cycles has been achieved in 23:1–25:18 and 35:23–36:43, but a systematic design is evident nonetheless. The two sections match up as follows:

A Death and burial of Sarah (23:1–20)
B Marriage of Isaac (24:1–67)
C Abraham's sons (25:1–6)
D Death and burial of Abraham (25:7–11)
E Ishmael's sons (25:12–18)
A′ ———
C′ Jacob's sons (35:23–26)
D′ Death and burial of Isaac (35:27–29)
B′ Marriages of Esau (36:1–5)
E′ Esau's sons (36:6–43)

Immediately we notice that the material in the second set duplicates to a great extent the material in the first set. But we also notice some imperfections, especially the lack of a corresponding A′ for A and the poor position of B′ between D′ and E′. Thus our previous statement that the aesthetic quality of the longer cycles is lacking in these chapters. But we should excuse our compiler, for he had before him more difficult material to work with. The flow of the Abraham and Jacob cycles could not be accomplished here given the long lists which dominate 23:1–25:18 and 35:23–36:43, especially the latter. Nevertheless, a redactional structure is achieved, and as the following unit-by-unit survey will show, the imperfections are explicable.

A DEATH AND BURIAL OF SARAH (23:1–20)

A′ ———

The death and burial of Sarah is not passed over in a simple notice (as is the case with others' deaths and burials; see below on D and D′), rather it is described in a fairly long pericope. It is all the more striking, therefore, that we have no parallel to it. The parallel we expect is the death and burial of Rebekah, but this is one of Genesis's most glaring lacunas. This matriarch's end goes unrecorded.

If we have learned anything in this investigation, it is that nothing is accidental in the redaction of Genesis. And thus we should expect a very good reason why Rebekah's death and burial are omitted.[1] The deception of Isaac, it will be recalled, was effectuated by two conspirators, Rebekah and Jacob. The latter receives his just desert in 29:25–26, illuminated by Laban's words *lōʾ yēʿāseh kēn bimqômēnû lātēt haṣṣᵉʿîrâ lipnê habbᵉkîrâ*, 'it is not the custom in our place to put the younger before the firstborn.'[2] But what about Rebekah? She after all was the instigator

[1] Passing reference is made later on, in 49:31, but it is inconsequential.

[2] See U. Cassuto, *The Documentary Hypothesis* (Jerusalem, 1961) 64; and R. Davidson, *Genesis 12–50* (Cambridge, 1979) 155.

in deceiving Isaac and thus we expect her deeds to be likewise recompensed.

Genesis is silent on this issue; but it is this very silence which is the key. Jacob's gaining the birthright and the blessing moves Esau to seek to kill him, and Jacob must flee to Haran. Never again in the narratives do we hear of Rebekah. The story continues to trace the life of Jacob, and we never again encounter his mother. We are left to conclude that she never saw her beloved son (see 25:28) again.[3] This was to be Rebekah's punishment, but it was one which she brought upon herself: *ʿālay qilᵉlātkā bᵉnî* 'upon me is your curse, my son,' she proclaims in 27:13. Clearly she must have died and been buried while Jacob was in Haran.[4] Accordingly, there is a very good explanation why Rebekah's death and burial receive no mention in Genesis.[5] The compiler sacrificed a more perfect redactional structure to drive home the point of Rebekah's punishment. As U. Cassuto said, "Undoubtedly a lesson that is taught by implication is capable of exerting a greater influence than one explicitly stated."[6]

B MARRIAGE OF ISAAC (24:1–67)
B′ MARRIAGES OF ESAU (36:1–5)

The marriage of Abraham's son, Isaac, is one of the largest units in all of Genesis. The marriages of Isaac's son, Esau, are of less concern to the biblical audience and

[3] Noted by D. Kidner, *Genesis* (Downers Grove, IL, 1967) 157. Cassuto (*Documentary Hypothesis*, 64) merely states that Rebekah's punishment was having to send "her dearly loved son away," but it is actually much greater.

[4] This is stated explicitly in Jubilees 35:27; Josephus, *Antiquities*, I.22.1; and in the few Midrashic sources cited by L. Ginzberg, *The Legends of the Jews* V (Philadelphia, 1953) 318, n 302.

[5] See further G. A. Rendsburg, "Notes on Genesis XXXV," *VT* 34 (1984) 361–65.

[6] Cassuto, *Documentary Hypothesis*, 63.

are therefore merely listed. But within the two linking sections, these units are parallel, a point which is brought out by two similarities.

i. In 24:3, 24:37, we read Abraham's instructions to his servant *lōʾ tiqqaḥ ʾiššâ libnî mibbᵉnôt hakkᵉnaᶜănî*, 'do not take a wife for my son from among the Canaanite women.' In 36:2 we read by contrast *ᶜēśāw lāqaḥ ʾet nāšāw mibbᵉnot kᵉnāᶜan*, 'Esau took his wives from among the Canaanite women.'

ii. On the other hand we have a correspondence, for Isaac and Esau both marry a cousin. In B it is Rebekah the daughter of Bethuel and sister of Laban; in B′ it is Basemath the daughter of Ishmael and sister of Nebaioth. Note that in each case paternal and fraternal references are made.

The marriages of Esau are obviously very much out of sequence, coming as they do between D′ and E′. But the redactor had very little choice, as he wished to present all the Esau-Edom material together. We will return to this problem below.

C ABRAHAM'S SONS (25:1–6)

C′ JACOB'S SONS (35:23–26)

Each section of linking material includes the sons of the patriarch who dominates the cycle just completed. Abraham's sons are not Ishmael, the one born to Hagar, and Isaac, the one born to Sarah, but the multiple children born to Keturah. This list is incorporated in 25:1–6 to more closely parallel the twelve children of Jacob in 35:23–26. The two units share two similarities.

i. *kol ʾēlleh bᵉnê qᵉṭûrâ*, 'all these are the sons of Keturah,' appears in 25:4; and *ʾēlleh bᵉnê yaᶜăqōb*, 'these are the sons of Jacob,' appears in 35:26.

ii. Keturah's sons live in *ʾereṣ qedem*, 'the land of Qedem,' in 25:6; and Jacob's sons are born in *paddan ʾărām*, 'Paddan Aram,' in 35:26. That these two geographic locales are equated in Genesis can be seen at 29:1.

By recognizing the parallel character of C and C′, we are perhaps able to shed light on a long standing crux in biblical studies. Scholars have noted that 35:23–26 places Benjamin's birth in Paddan Aram, at variance with 35:16–18 which has him born in Canaan. No sound explanation for this problem has been forthcoming except to say that Benjamin "must be tacitly excepted"[7] or to ascribe variant traditions to different sources.[8] But it is also possible that Benjamin is included in this list to place all of Jacob's sons in Mesopotamia, the domain of Abraham's sons through Keturah.

D DEATH AND BURIAL OF ABRAHAM (25:7–11)

D′ DEATH AND BURIAL OF ISAAC (35:27–29)

Many scholars have noted the similarity between these two units, including the various theme-words and phrases which highlight the correspondence.[9]

i. The ages of the patriarchs are given in 25:7 and 35:28.
ii. In 25:8 we read *wayyigwaᶜ wayyāmot ᵓabrāhām*, 'Abraham expired and died'; and in 35:29 we have *wayyigwaᶜ yiṣḥāq wayyāmot*, 'Isaac expired and died.'
iii. The root *śbᶜ*, 'full,' is used in 25:8 and 35:29.
iv. *wayyēᵓāsep ᵓel ᶜammāw*, 'he was gathered unto his people,' occurs in 25:8 and 35:29.
v. *wayyiqbᵉrû ᵓōtô*, 'they buried him,' is predicated of Abraham's two sons, in 25:9 and of Isaac's two sons in 35:29.
vi. Mamre appears in 25:9 and 35:27.

[7] S. R. Driver, *The Book of Genesis* (London, 1906) 312; similarly B. Jacob, *Das erste Buch der Tora: Genesis* (Berlin, 1934) 669.

[8] E. A. Speiser, *Genesis* (Garden City, NY, 1964) 273.

[9] Driver, *The Book of Genesis*, 312; Jacob, *Das erste Buch der Tora: Genesis*, 669; Speiser, *Genesis*, 273; Davidson, *Genesis 12–50*, 205; B. Vawter, *On Genesis* (Garden City, NY, 1977) 366; and J. Skinner, *Genesis* (New York, 1910) 428.

E ISHMAEL'S SONS (25:12–18)
E′ ESAU'S SONS (36:6–43)

Commentators on Genesis have also noted that these units parallel each other.[10] The story of the first patriarch is complete, and before moving on to the Isaac and Jacob material in 25:19–35:22 the redactor included Ishmael's family tree to close the book on Abraham. Similarly, the story of Isaac is over, and before moving on to the Jacob and Joseph material in 37:1–50:26 the redactor incorporated detailed material on Esau to close the book on the second patriarch's family. The analagous units share one expression which further link the two lists.

i. *wᵉʾēlleh šᵉmôt bᵉnê yišmāʿēʾl*, 'and these are the names of Ishmael's sons,' in 25:13, is paralleled by *ʾēlleh šᵉmôt bᵉnê ʿēśāw*, 'these are the names of Esau's sons,' in 36:10.

OVERVIEW

The material in 23:1–25:18 which links the Abraham and Jacob Cycles is paralleled in 35:23-36:43 which links the Jacob and Joseph Cycles. The correspondences are not always perfect, but the redactor has attempted to bring them together nonetheless. For example, in B it is Abraham's chief heir, Isaac, who marries; but in B′ it is a secondary character, Isaac's son Esau, who marries. The story of the marriage(s) of Isaac's chief heir, Jacob, would be hopelessly out of place here, because it played such an important role in the Jacob Cycle itself. So the redactor limited himself to dealing with Esau's marriages here, which, as noted above, explains why B′ is apparently misplaced. It logically belongs before E′, the list of Esau's sons, regardless of the redactional structure. Again, we may excuse our redactor whose task was most difficult in aligning these units.

[10] Driver, *The Book of Genesis*, 312; Jacob, *Das erste Buch der Tora: Genesis*, 671; and Davidson, *Genesis 12–50*, 208.

The imperfect correspondences of 23:1–28:18 and 35:23–36:43 are also evident from the fact that Abraham in A through E is usually paralleled by Isaac in A′ through E′ but once by Jacob. That is to say, it is Abraham's son who marries in B and Isaac's son who marries in B′; it is Abraham who is buried in D and Isaac who is buried in D′; it is Abraham's son Ishmael who is the subject of E and it is Isaac's son Esau who is the subject of E′; and it is Abraham's wife Sarah who dies in A and presumably Isaac's wife Rebekah who dies in the glaringly absent A′. But C concerns Abraham's sons while C′ concerns Jacob's sons. Obviously, the compiler had no choice, for Isaac simply did not have a multitude of sons from another woman. Instead, he inserted a list of Jacob's numerous sons here, and cemented the relationship between C and C′ by utilizing the resemblances discussed above.

Finally, let it be noted, as was done at the end of chap. II, that the units of A through E exactly equal the rabbinic Parshat Ḥayye Sarah. The rabbis recognized 23:1–25:18 as an independent section, attaching it neither to the Abraham Cycle which precedes it nor to the Jacob Cycle which follows it. 35:23–36:43 is much shorter in length, so it could not stand as its own division of the Torah in the traditional Jewish reading cycle. Accordingly, it forms the end of Parshat Wayyishlaḥ.

V

THE JOSEPH STORY

The fourth and last major cycle in the book of Genesis is the Joseph Story. It is, by all accounts, the most unified story in Genesis, perhaps in the entire Pentateuch, and indeed in the whole Hebrew Bible. John Skinner called it "the most artistic and most fascinating of OT biographies";[1] G. von Rad described it as "an organically constructed narrative;"[2] and Nahum Sarna spoke of its "unparalleled continuity of narrative."[3] It has been labeled a "romance,"[4] a "short novel,"[5] and a "Märchen-Novella."[6] True to its Egyptian setting, the Joseph Story's literary genre is similar to the Middle and Late Egyptian stories centering on the trials and tribulations of the hero who eventually meets with success. Like Sinuhe, Shipwrecked Sailor, Eloquent Peasant, Tale of Two Brothers, and Wenamon, to a great extent the Joseph Story is literature for literature's sake.[7]

If the first three cycles in Genesis, whose finished products are collections of various traditions brought together, reveal redactional structuring, it is not surprising to find a similar system operating in the Joseph Cycle.

[1] J. Skinner, *Genesis* (New York, 1910) 438.

[2] G. von Rad, *Genesis* (Philadelphia, 1961) 342.

[3] N. M. Sarna, *Understanding Genesis* (New York, 1966) 211.

[4] H. Gunkel, *The Legends of Genesis* (New York, 1964) 79–80.

[5] R. Davidson, *Genesis 12–50* (Cambridge, 1979) 212.

[6] D. B. Redford, *A Study of the Biblical Story of Joseph* (Leiden, 1970) 66–68.

[7] Redford, *A Study of the Biblical Story of Joseph*, 66–68; and C. H. Gordon, *The Common Background of Greek and Hebrew Civilizations* (New York, 1965), passim but especially 103.

This holds not only for the chapters dealing with Joseph directly, but for the material in which he is absent or nominally present as well. I refer, of course, to the interruptions of 38:1–30 and 49:1–28. The Judah and Tamar episode and Jacob's testament are interludes which break up the telling of the Joseph Story, but they nevertheless have been skillfully worked into the redactional plan of the cycle.

The structure of the Joseph Story is as follows:

A Joseph and his brothers, Jacob and Joseph part (37:1–36)
B Interlude: Joseph not present (38:1–30)
C Reversal: Joseph guilty, Potiphar's wife innocent (39:1–23)
D Joseph hero of Egypt (40:1–41:57)
E Two trips to Egypt (42:1–43:34)
F Final test (44:1–34)
F′ Conclusion of Test (45:1–28)
E′ Two tellings of migration to Egypt (46:1–47:12)
D′ Joseph hero of Egypt (47:13–27)
C′ Reversal: Ephraim firstborn, Manasseh secondborn (47:28–48:22)
B′ Interlude: Joseph nominally present (49:1–28)
A′ Joseph and his brothers, Jacob and Joseph part (49:29–50:26)

As with the Abraham Cycle and the Jacob Cycle, the Joseph Story builds to a pivot point after which the themes and stories are repeated in reverse order. There are six episodes (A, B, C, D, E, F) leading to the climax of the novella; then follow six parallel episodes (F′, E′, D′, C′, B′, A′). The result is a neatly constructed palistrophe in what is already a remarkably unified story.

A JOSEPH AND HIS BROTHERS; JACOB AND JOSEPH PART (37:1–36)

A′ JOSEPH AND HIS BROTHERS; JACOB AND JOSEPH PART (49:29–50:26)

These two units act as the introduction and conclusion to the Joseph Story. In A we meet Joseph for the first time (excluding his birth in 30:22–24) as a 17-year-old *naʿar*.[8] In A′ he appears as trusted advisor to Pharaoh who lives the full life of 110 years.[9] The contrast is striking and illustrates the rise in Joseph's career.

The action of A is repeated in A′ in two major ways. In both sections Joseph is alone with his brothers, their father Jacob not part of the scene. Also, in A father and son part due to the faked death of the latter, and in A′ father and son part due to the actual death of the former.

A whole host of theme-words link the episodes still further.

i. In 37:1 we read that Jacob lived *b^{e}ʾereṣ m^{e}gûrê ʾabîw*, 'in the land of his father's sojourning'; and in 49:29 the patriarch instructs Joseph *qibrû ʾōtî ʾel ʾăbōtāy*, 'bury me with my fathers.'

ii. *b^{e}ʾereṣ k^{e}nāʿan*, 'in the land of Canaan,' occurs in 37:1; and *ʾarṣāh k^{e}nāʿan*, 'to the land of Canaan,' occurs in 50:13.

iii. The word *rāʿâ*, 'evil,' appears frequently in both units, in 37:2, 37:20, 37:33, and in 50:15, 50:17, 50:20.

iv. *ʾăbîhem*, 'their father,' is also prominent in both A and A′, occurring in 37:2, 37:4, 37:12, 37:32 and in 49:28, 50:15.

v. In 37:4 we read *wayyirʾû ʾeḥāw*, 'his brothers saw'; and in 50:15 we have *wayyirʾû ʾăḥê yôsēp*, 'Joseph's brothers saw.'

vi. The verbal root *dbr*, 'speak,' is used in A in 37:4 and commonly in A′ in 49:28, 50:4 (bis), 50:17, 50:21.

vii. In 37:7, 37:9, 37:10, the Hištaphʿel (Št) of *ḥwh*, 'prostrate,'[10] is used in Joseph's dreams to illustrate his

[8] However this ambiguous word is to be translated in this context (*NAB*: 'assistant'; *NJPSV*: 'helper'), one of its connotations is that of a young boy. See especially Exod 2:6 where the 3-month-old Moses is called a *naʿar*.

[9] On this as the ideal age of an Egyptian, see J. M. A. Janssen, "On the Ideal Lifetime of the Egyptian," *OMRO* 31 (1950) 33–44.

[10] For this grammatical analysis of *hištaḥ^{a}weh*, etc., see C. H. Gordon, *Ugaritic Textbook* (Rome, 1967) 395; and the many works cited by J. A. Emerton, "The Etymology of *hištaḥ^{a}wāh*," in *Instruction and*

brothers' obeisance; this reverberates with *wayyippᵉlû lᵉpānāw*, 'they (his brothers) fell before him (Joseph),' in 50:18.

viii. *wayyelᵉkû (gam) ʾeḥāw*, 'his brothers went,' occurs in 37:12 and 50:18.

ix. A local man assists Joseph in 37:15–17 and the local Canaanites witness Joseph's and his entourage's mourning in 50:11.

x. The verbal root *nkl* in the Hithpaᶜel, 'plot,' is used in 37:18, and the non-related but assonant root *klkl*, 'sustain,' is used in 50:21.

xi. Similarly, the verbal root *nkr*, 'recognize,' is predicated of Jacob in 37:32–33, and Joseph reports Jacob's use of *karîtî*, 'I dug,' from the non-related but assonant root *krh* in 50:5.

xii. The root *ʾbl*, 'mourn,' is used in connection with Jacob's mourning for Joseph in 37:34–35, and in 50:10–11 in connection with Joseph's mourning for Jacob.

Throughout this work we have demonstrated how attention to redactional structuring can help explain many problems raised by critics, especially those concerning supposed secondary accretions to the text. Another example of this is the admittedly peculiar reference to the unnamed stranger who assists Joseph in his search for his brothers. Gerhard von Rad and Donald Redford have labeled 37:15–17 specifically "secondary,"[11] but a closer look reveals that it is integral. It is needed to counterbalance the reference to the local Canaanites in 50:11. Redford also considers the latter verse secondary,[12] but it is odd that both "secondary" additions are among the points which cement the bond between A and A′.

Interpretation (*OTS* 20; Leiden, 1977) 41–55, especially 42. I disagree with Emerton's conclusions, but his presentation of the material is first-class.

[11] Von Rad, *Genesis*, 347; and Redford, *A Study of the Biblical Story of Joseph*, 145.

[12] Redford, *A Study of the Biblical Story of Joseph*, 246.

B INTERLUDE: JOSEPH NOT PRESENT (38:1–30)

B′ INTERLUDE: JOSEPH NOMINALLY PRESENT (49:1–28)

It hardly takes deep analysis into the Joseph Story to realize that B is a unit with no direct relationship to the general story line. Joseph is nowhere mentioned, and although there are connections between B and A and C (see below), the narrative is complete without 38:1–30. That this chapter is an interlude has not only been recognized by modern scholars,[13] but by Rashi and Ibn Ezra centuries ago.

Although it has been worked into the story a bit more directly, B′ is also an interlude. It interrupts the narrative, as a comparison of 48:21–22 and 49:29 exhibits. Joseph is only nominally present, unlike C′ and A′ where he dominates. 49:1–27 is clearly an independent poem. Redford has astutely noted that it is set in Canaan,[14] and in this sense it is a fitting parallel to 38:1–30 which deals with Judah's life in the same country. The Egyptian flavor which characterizes the Joseph Story is lacking in both units.

The Judah and Tamar episode and the Testament of Jacob might seem too different—beyond their role as interludes and their setting in Canaan—to have themes and theme-words linking them in any meaningful way. But such is not the case, for as the following list indicates, there are surprisingly more such items shared by B and B′ than by any other matching units in the cycle.

[13] Von Rad, *Genesis*, 351; Davidson, *Genesis 12–50*, 224; B. Vawter, *On Genesis* (Garden City, NY, 1977), 389; E. A. Speiser, *Genesis* (Garden City, NY, 1964), 299; Redford, *A Study of the Biblical Story of Joseph*, 16–18; and J. Goldin, "The Youngest Son or Where Does Genesis 38 Belong," *JBL* 96 (1977) 27.

[14] Redford, *A Study of the Biblical Story of Joseph*, 25. Also pertinent are B. Vawter, "The Canaanite Background of Genesis 49," *CBQ* 17 (1955) 1–18; and J. Coppens, "La Bénédiction de Jacob," *Volume du Congrès Strasbourg* (*VTSup* 4; Leiden, 1957) 97–115.

Since the only common material in B and B′ is that concerning Judah, it is appropriate to begin by looking at Jacob's words to his fourth son in 49:8–12. These verses are filled with cruxes, but scholars in the last twenty years have begun to solve some of them by reading them as references to the Judah and Tamar episode. From the works of Edwin Good,[15] Calum Carmichael,[16] and James Ackerman[17] the following tie-ins may be cited.

i. The key to seeing the blessing to Judah as a reference to 38:1–30 is the similarity between *šîlōh*, traditionally rendered 'Shiloh,' in 49:10, and *šēlâ*, 'Shelah,' in 38:5, 38:11, 38:14, 38:26.[18]

ii. The *šēbet*, 'sceptre,' shall not depart from Judah in 49:10, just as Judah's *maṭṭeh*, 'staff,' was handed to Tamar in 38:18 and used as evidence against him in 38:25.

iii. A sexual connotation can certainly be read into *meḥōqēq mibbên raglāw*, 'the staff between his legs,' in 49:10, and allied to Judah's visiting a prostitute in 38:15–19.

iv. *ʿîrōh*, 'his donkey,' in 49:11, evokes *ʿēr*, 'Er,' Judah's first son in 38:3, 38:6, 38:7.

v. Similarly, *b^enî ʾătōnô*, 'son of his she-ass,' in 49:11, brings to mind *ʾônān*, 'Onan,' Judah's second son in 38:4, 38:8, 38:9.

[15] E. M. Good, "The 'Blessing' on Judah, Gen. 49:8–12," *JBL* 82 (1963) 427–32.

[16] C. M. Carmichael, "Some Sayings in Genesis 49," *JBL* 88 (1969) 435–44 especially 439–41.

[17] J. S. Ackerman, "Joseph, Judah and Jacob," in *Literary Interpretations of Biblical Narratives* II (ed. K. R. R. Gros Louis; Nashville, 1982) 111.

[18] A possible connection between Shiloh and Shelah has been noted earlier by H. E. Ryle, *The Book of Genesis* (Cambridge, 1914) 431; Skinner, *Genesis*, 520, 524; A. B. Ehrlich, *Randglossen zur hebräischen Bibel* I (Leipzig, 1908) 246; W. Schröder, "Gen 49:10, Versuch einer Erklärung," *ZAW* 29 (1909) 194–95; W. H. Bennett, *Genesis* (Edinburgh, 1904) 397; and B. Jacob, *Das erste Buch der Tora: Genesis* (Berlin, 1934) 907. This interpretation may already have been in the minds of the translator of Targum Jonathan which reads *zʿyr bnwy*, 'his youngest son,' and Qimḥi and other medieval exegetes who accept this understanding of Masoretic *šylh*.

vi. *śōrēqâ*, 'vine, stock,' in 49:11, alludes to the valley of Soreq, which recalls Timnah in 38:12–13.[19]

Other links between the blessing to Judah and his earlier escapades may also be pointed out.

vii. The verbal root *swr* in the Qal, 'depart,' appears in 49:10; and in the Hiphᶜil, 'remove,' it occurs in 38:14, 38:19.

viii. *yābōᵓ*, 'he comes,' in 49:10, suggests *wayyābōᵓ*, 'he came,' in 38:18.

ix. *sûtōh*, 'his robe,' in 49:11, is not etymologically related to *kissᵉtâ*, 'she covered,' in 38:15, but they share three consonants, sound alike, and both convey the idea of clothing.

x. The root *lbš*, 'clothe,' appears in both 49:11 and 38:19.

The few verses spoken to Judah thus contain ten theme-words which link B′ with Judah's history in B. But the blessings to the other sons also contain similar expressions to those in 38:1–30.

xi. *bᵉkôr*, 'firstborn,' occurs in 49:3 and 38:6.

xii. *ᵓônî*, 'my vigor,' in 49:3, might also suggest *ᵓônān*, 'Onan,' in 38:4, 38:8, 38:9.

xiii. The word *ᶜāz*, 'strong, fierce,' is used in 49:3, 49:7; and in 38:17, 38:20, we have *ᶜizzîm*, 'goats.'

[19] This point is noted only by Ackerman ("Joseph, Judah, and Jacob," 111) who states unequivocally that Timnah "is located in the valley of Sorek ('vineyard')." Ackerman has in mind the Timnah of Judg 14:1, though actually the Timnah of 38:12–13 is probably another Timnah, higher in the Judean hills; see Skinner, *Genesis*, 453; Jacob, *Das erste Buch der Tora: Genesis*, 714; S. R. Driver, *The Book of Genesis* (London, 1906) 329; von Rad, *Genesis*, 354; Davidson, *Genesis 12–50*, 228; and A. Dillmann, *Genesis* II (Edinburgh, 1897) 346. But this does not mean that the *śōrēqâ*/Timnah parallel between B and B′ fails. The Hebrew reader, not conscious to identify every geographic locale specifically, might easily have thought of the Timnah of 38:12–13 as the Timnah in the Soreq Valley. We may even ask whether it is relevant that two of Samson's loves are his unnamed fiancée of Timnah (Judges 14) and Delilah of the Soreq Valley (Judges 16).

xiv. *wayyēṭ* is used in 49:15 and in 38:16 meaning 'he bent, he turned'; and it also occurs in 38:1 meaning 'he pitched.'

xv. In 49:17 we read *ᶜălê derek*, 'by the road'; and in 38:16 we have *ʾel hadderek*, 'by the road.'

xvi. The alliteration *gād gᵉdûd yᵉgûdennû*, 'Gad shall be raided by raiders,' in 49:19, suggests the important *gᵉdî* 'kid,' in 38:17, 38:20, 38:23.

xvii. *yāgud*, 'he shall raid,' in 49:19, evokes *wayyuggad*, 'it was told,' in 38:24.

In sum, there are seventeen theme-words which highlight the parallel status of 38:1–30 and 49:1–28. As a comparison with other matching units in this Cycle or in other Cycles will determine, seventeen such parallels is an unusually high number. Perhaps because the Judah and Tamar episode and the Testament of Jacob are so dissimilar, the need was felt for more shared words and ideas than is customary. That is to say, A and A′ and the other matching units of the Joseph Story are similar enough in action not to require that many theme-words. B and B′ are less homogeneous, however, and thus the redactor has insured their correspondence through a veritable plethora of theme-words. Commentators have usually dismissed the two pericopes as interludes, which is here not denied, but they should also be recognized as the balancing second and penultimate sections in the Joseph Story. As such, they are similar to 26:1–34 and 34:1–31, interluding second and penultimate stories in the Jacob Cycle (discussed above in chap. III).

C REVERSAL: JOSEPH GUILTY, POTIPHAR'S WIFE INNOCENT (39:1–23)

C′ REVERSAL: EPHRAIM FIRSTBORN, MANASSEH SECONDBORN (47:28–48:22)

In the first of these chapters, a switch of positions finds Joseph, who is innocent, found guilty, and Potiphar's wife, who in actuality is guilty, found innocent. In the second episode, Ephraim, who actually is the secondborn, is declared the firstborn, and Manasseh, who naturally is the firstborn, is reduced to the secondborn. In both instances, Joseph's superior is ultimately responsible for the reversals whether it be his master Potiphar or his father Jacob. In each case the action centers around the bed. This is explicit in C′ where Jacob lies in bed (*miṭṭâ* in 47:31) and Joseph is beside him, and implicit in C where Potiphar's wife presumably is in bed or has the bed in mind and Joseph is beside her.

A series of theme-words link the two units.

i. The verbal root *brk*, 'bless,' is important in both units, occurring in 39:5 (bis) and in 48:3, 48:9, 48:15, 48:16, 48:20 (bis).

ii. *wayᵉmāʾēn wayyōʾmer*, 'he resisted and said,' appears in 39:8; and the same words with the subject *ʾābîw*, 'his father,' interposed occur in 48:19.

iii. In 39:4 we read *wayyimṣāʾ yôsēp ḥēn bᵉʿênāw*, 'Joseph found favor in his eyes'; and in 47:29 we have *ʾim nāʾ māṣāʾtî ḥēn bᵉʿênekā*, 'if I have found favor in your eyes.'

iv. The word *ḥesed*, 'favor,' is used in both 39:21 and 47:29.

v. The verbal root *škb*, 'lie,' is prominent in C, occurring four times in 39:7–14, and it reverberates in C′ in 47:30.

vi. *yād*, 'hand,' in its various forms, is extremely common and very important in C, occurring nine times.[20] It is equally important to C′ since the reversal results from Jacob's crossed hands and because it is used in Joseph's swearing to Jacob; see 47:29, 48:14, 48:17 (bis).

vii. *leḥem*, literally 'bread' but figuratively 'wife'[21] occurs in 39:6; and *bêt lāḥem*, 'Bethlehem (house of bread),' occurs in 48:7.

[20] On the use of *yād*, 'hand,' in its various forms, in the story of Joseph, Potiphar, and Potiphar's wife, see the insightful treatment by R. Alter, *The Art of Biblical Narrative* (New York, 1981) 107–11. Alter calls such a word, which we label "theme-word," a *Leitwort*, having borrowed the term from M. Buber, *Werker* II, *Schriften zur Bibel* (Munich, 1964) 1131 (originally published with F. Rosenweig as the preface to their German translation of the Bible in the 1920s and 1930s).

[21] For this understanding of *leḥem*, obvious from a comparison with 39:9, one must consult the medieval Jewish exegetes (Rashi, Ibn

Once more recognition of redactional structuring allows us to solve a problem which has plagued scholars. Von Rad,[22] Davidson,[23] Vawter,[24] and Skinner[25] all note that the reference to Rachel's death and burial in 48:7 is seemingly out of place or poorly related to the general context. August Dillmann was less concerned about the notice as a whole, stating that "the absence of any apparent motive prevents our regarding the verse as a mere gloss," but he did note that "the words *hwʾ byt lḥm* are out of place in Jacob's mouth, and are a late addition."[26] Admittedly this is correct, for one would not expect to see such a gloss (see Genesis 14 for many more examples) in direct speech. But by paying heed to the use of *leḥem* in C in 39:6, where it is pregnant with meaning, we are able to uncover our author's or compiler's reason for including *bêt lāḥem* in C′ in 48:7. The two act as theme-words which serve to cement the relationship between the two units.

D JOSEPH HERO OF EGYPT (40:1–41:57)
D′ JOSEPH HERO OF EGYPT (47:13–27)

Twice during the Joseph Story we have episodes which describe how Joseph saves Egypt from famine and becomes a national hero. It is clear that these units, one

---

Ezra, Qimḥi, and others) who derive their knowledge ultimately from Bereshit Rabbah 86:6 and Targum Yerushalmi to Genesis 39:6. None of the modern commentators, save Jacob (*Das erste Buch der Tora: Genesis*, 728), mentions this. For another example of *leḥem* = 'wife, woman' see Exod 2:20; see also Shabbat 62b and Ketubot 13a in the Talmud.

[22] Von Rad (*Genesis*, 410) writes: "The reference to Rachel's death has no recognizable relation to what follows or precedes."

[23] Davidson (*Genesis 12–50*, 294) writes: "This brief note about the death and burial of Rachel (see 35:16–20) is poorly related to the context. . . . What is not clear is why it appears at this point in Jacob's speech to Joseph."

[24] Vawter (*On Genesis*, 452) calls it "a seemingly pointless reference to Rachel's death and burial."

[25] Skinner (*Genesis*, 504–5) writes: "The notice . . . is very loosely connected with what precedes."

[26] Dillmann, *Genesis* II, 437–38.

relatively long and one relatively short, are parallel. The following theme-words highlight the correspondence.

i. The word *rāᶜāb*, 'famine,' occurs ubiquitously in D and in D′ in 47:13 (bis), 47:20.
ii. The word *leḥem*, 'bread,' is used twice in D in 41:54–55, and commonly in D′.
iii. (*wᵉ*)*tālâ*, 'he hung/will hang,' occurs in 40:19, 40:22, and *wattēlah*, 'languished,' appears in 47:13.
iv. The verbal root *šbr*, 'buy/sell grain,' is used in 41:56–57 and in 47:14; the noun *šeber*, 'grain,' also occurs in 47:14.
v. *qāneh*, 'stalk,' appears in 41:5, 41:22, and the verbal root *qnh*, 'buy,' occurs in 47:19, 47:22, 47:23.
vi. *ᶜārîm*, 'cities,' is used in 41:48 and 47:21.
vii. *ᵓereṣ miṣrayim*, 'the land of Egypt,' or simply *hāᵓāreṣ*, 'the land,' are exceedingly common in D and D′; the latter also uses *ᵓădāmâ*, 'land,' and various forms.
viii. The root *ḥmš* in the sense of dividing the land into fifths occurs in 41:34 and 47:24, 47:26.

The similarity between 40:1–41:57 and 47:13–27 is obvious and these shared theme-words only heighten the correspondence. Moreover, attention to the redactional structure of the Joseph Story obviates the difficulty sensed by Redford that the story of the agrarian reforms in 47:13–27 is extraneous to the cycle.[27] Not so, however, for it is needed to counterbalance the episode of 40:1–41:57 where Joseph first appears as the hero of Egypt.

E TWO TRIPS TO EGYPT (42:1–43:34)

E′ TWO TELLINGS OF MIGRATION TO EGYPT (46:1–47:12)

As the Joseph Story progresses there follows the account of the brothers' two trips to Egypt. In the first trip they go merely to acquire food and in the second trip they return with Benjamin in order to free Simeon. Parallel to the two journeys are two tellings of how Jacob's family migrates to Egypt and settles in Goshen. The first

[27] Redford, *A Study of the Biblical Story of Joseph*, 180.

account is comprised mainly of a genealogical list and the second describes the presentation of Jacob and his sons before Pharaoh.

Various items link the two units.

i. In 42:1–2, *r^e^dû*, 'go down,' and *miṣrayim*, 'Egypt,' are collocated; in 46:3 we read *mêr^e^dâ miṣraymāh*, 'from going down to Egypt.'

ii. The brothers present themselves as *ʿăbādekā*, 'your servants,' to Joseph in 42:10, 42:11, 42:13, and use the same term in speaking to Pharaoh in 46:34, 47:3, 47:4 (bis).

iii. Judah has a prominent role in 43:3–10, and he appears in 46:28 as well.

iv. The verbal root *šlḥ*, 'send,' is used in connection with Jacob sending his sons led by Judah to Egypt in 43:4–5, and in 46:28 when he sends Judah ahead to pave the way.

v. *lōʾ tirʾû pānay*, 'you shall not see my face,' are Joseph's words quoted to Jacob in 43:5; and *r^e^ʾōtî ʾet pānekā*, 'I have seen your face,' are Jacob's words to Joseph in 46:30.

vi. Similarly, *haʿôd ʾăbîkem ḥay*, 'is your father still alive?' are Joseph's words quoted to Jacob in 43:7; and *kî ʿôd^e^kā ḥāy*, 'that you are still alive,' are Jacob's words to Joseph in 46:30.

Again we are able to alleviate a problem sensed by Redford by paying heed to redactional structuring. Redford opined that 46:1–27 is secondary to the cycle: "With the beginning of chapter 46 the reader has momentarily taken leave of the Joseph Story. . . . It is clear, then, that these verses do not belong to the Joseph Story."[28] But, since there are *two* journeys which the brothers make in E, there need to be *two* descriptions of the final migration to Egypt in E′. Since there was only one actual migration

[28] Redford, *A Study of the Biblical Story of Joseph*, 18–22, especially 18–19. Other scholars (Davidson, *Genesis 12–50*, 279; von Rad, *Genesis*, 397; Vawter, *On Genesis*, 441; Speiser, *Genesis*, 346–47) write similarly concerning only 46:6–27, pointing to a presumed continuity between 46:5 and 46:28 as proof.

by Jacob's family, the compiler could only give one account, to wit, 46:28–47:12. But to balance the two actual journeys of 42:1–43:34,[29] our redactor incorporated a brief notice about a theophany discussing the descent followed by a long genealogy describing the extent of the family which settled in Egypt. That we indeed have two accounts of the one migration may be clearly seen by comparing 46:6 *wayyabōʾû miṣraymāh*, 'they came to Egypt,' (see also 46:8, 46:27) with 46:28 *wayyabōʾû ʾarṣāh gôšen*, 'they came to the land of Goshen.'

F FINAL TEST (44:1–34)

F′ CONCLUSION OF TEST (45:1–28)

Standing at the middle of the Joseph Story are the unit leading up to the cycle's denouement and the denouement itself. The former is highlighted by Judah's famous speech, unsurpassed in Scripture for the sympathy and suffering, emotion and pathos it stirs. Indeed it moves Joseph to tears and to disclose his true identity, actions which dominate the latter unit.

F and F′ are further connected by the following theme-words:

i. The verbal root *mhr*, 'hasten,' occurs in 44:11 and in 45:9, 45:13.
ii. *pî*, 'mouth of,' occurs in the sense of the mouth of the bag in 44:1, 44:2, 44:8 and in the sense of a human mouth in 45:12, 45:21.
iii. Benjamin is essential to F, mentioned specifically in 44:12 and alluded to as the youngest brother throughout Judah's speech in 44:18–34; he is also notable in F′ in 45:12, 45:14, 45:22.
iv. The verbal root *šlḥ*, 'send,' appears in F in 44:3 and commonly, six times to be exact, in F′.
v. The verbal root *yrd*, 'descend,' is common in F, occurring seven times, and appears in F′ in 45:9, 45:13.

[29] As Redford (*A Study of the Biblical Story of Joseph*, 74–75) notes, duplicate episodes are a major literary feature of the Joseph Story.

vi. Judah describes Jacob's reaction to Joseph's absence and presumed death in 44:28 *ṭārōp ṭōrāp*, 'he must have been torn to pieces'; Joseph lets his brothers know that he knows the true story in 45:5 *m^ekartem ʾōtî*, 'you sold me.'

OVERVIEW

Like the second and third cycles of Genesis, the Joseph Story contains a series of units building toward a climax, then follows a second series where matching units in reverse order bring the story to resolution and fulfillment.[30] The pivot point stands precisely in the center of the cycle, 45:1–4, where Joseph reveals himself to his brothers. Everything in A through F (with the possible exception of the interlude in B) has been structured to put Joseph in the position of power whereby he can exact playful revenge on his brothers. From F′ through A′ (perhaps even including the interlude in B′) all is resolved. Jacob's family migrates to Egypt and settles in Goshen, famine strikes, yet Joseph sustains the people, Joseph's children receive Jacob's blessing, Jacob breathes his last breath, and Joseph too dies, having lived the fullest of lives as indicated by his 110-year life-span. Our redactor

[30] I should state here that a literary analysis of the Cycle has also been attempted by G. W. Coats, *From Canaan to Egypt* (Washington, DC, 1976) 7–55 (an expansion of his earlier article "Redactional Unity in Genesis 37–50," *JBL* 93 [1974] 15–21). I make no attempt to dovetail my analysis of the symmetry of the Joseph Story with that of Coats, for we differ on one major point. The basis for my study is the finished product, i.e., all of chapters 37–50. Coats, on the other hand, limits himself to 37, 39:1–47:27, considering 38 "not an intrinsic element in the Joseph story" and 47:28–50:26 to be "a framework narrative" and thus exclusive of "the primary structure of the Joseph story"; see *From Canaan to Egypt*, 8, n 3. The entire Cycle has been treated from a literary perspective by D. A. Seybold, "Paradox and Symmetry in the Joseph Narrative," in *Literary Interpretations of Biblical Narratives* (ed. K. R. R. Gros Louis; Nashville, 1974) 59–73. I accept many of Seybold's conclusions as well as the entire thrust of his article. It should be pointed out that his study upsets none of my conclusions nor does my study contradict any of his.

has done his job remarkably well, even to the very last word of Genesis, *b^emiṣrāyim*, 'in Egypt,' a fitting conclusion to the Joseph Story which also neatly sets the scene for the book of Exodus.[31]

As with the other major cycles of Genesis, so here there also obtain catchwords or nexuses which link successive units. These are most prominent between A and B and between B and C, the result of B's role as a strange interlude in the Joseph Story. That is to say, because B is not directly related to the main narrative, it was important for the compiler to include as many bridges as possible in order to link the Judah and Tamar episode with the novella of Joseph and his brothers. The most illustrative of the nexuses between A and B was already noted by R. Yohanan in Bereshit Rabbah 85:2 and repeated by countless modern scholars.[32]

i. *hakker nāʾ . . . wayyakkîrāh*, '"recognize please" . . . and he recognized it,' occurs in 37:32–33; and *hakker nāʾ . . . wayyakkēr*, '"recognize please" . . . and he recognized,' occurs in 38:25–26.

U. Cassuto and John Emerton take this analogy one step further noting the following similarity.[33]

ii. The twofold use of *nkr*, 'recognize,' is preceded by the root *šlḥ*, 'send,' in 37:32 and 38:25.

U. Cassuto, writing almost 60 years ago,[34] and Robert Alter, writing very recently (and apparently unaware of

[31] This point has been duly noted by Skinner, *Genesis*, 540; Jacob, *Das Erste Buch der Tora: Genesis*, 945; and Speiser, *Genesis*, lx, 378.

[32] Jacob, *Das erste Buch der Tora: Genesis*, 724; Redford, *A Study of the Biblical Story of Joseph*, 18; Coats, "Redactional Unity in Genesis 37–50," 17; Goldin, "The Youngest Son or Where Does Genesis 38 Belong," 29; J. A. Emerton, "Some Problems in Genesis XXXVIII," *VT* 25 (1975) 347; Alter, *The Art of Biblical Narrative*, 10; and U. Cassuto, "The Story of Judah and Tamar," in *Biblical and Oriental Studies* (Jerusalem, 1973 [original Hebrew 1929]) 30–31.

[33] Cassuto, "The Story of Judah and Tamar," 30–31; and Emerton, "Some Problems in Genesis XXXVIII," 347.

[34] U. Cassuto, "The Story of Judah and Tamar," 30–31 and 31, n 6.

Cassuto's article),[35] adduced many more catchwords and similar ideas which link A and B.

iii. The root *nḥm*, 'console,' is used in 37:35 and 38:12.
iv. *ś*^{e}*ʿîr ʿizzîm*, 'goat' (literally 'buck of the goats') occurs in 37:31; and *g*^{e}*dî ʿizzîm*, 'kid' (literally 'kid of the goats') occurs in 38:17.
v. Joseph's dreams in A reflect the reversal of the rule of primogeniture; the outcome of the Judah and Tamar episode includes the same motif.
vi. Jacob is deceived specifically by a piece of clothing in A, as is Judah in B.
vii. It is Judah who suggests selling Joseph which leads to the deception of Jacob; thus it is only fitting that it is Judah who is duped as the story progresses.[36]
viii. A striking contrast reveals Jacob mourning deeply over the imagined loss of Joseph, with no response whatsoever from Judah over the actual deaths of Er and Onan.

Links between B and C are fewer in number but no less important. R. Lazar in Bereshit Rabbah 85:2, Rashi in the medieval period,[37] and some moderns[38] noted the first of these.

i. The root *yrd*, 'descend,' occurs at the start of each unit, in 38:1 and 39:1.

R. Samuel bar Nahman in the same midrash, Ibn Ezra in the medieval period,[39] and some moderns[40] noted the second such bridge.

[35] Alter, *The Art of Biblical Narrative*, 6–10.

[36] The notion of the deceiver deceived is noted by Redford (*A Study of the Biblical Story of Joseph*, 18) too.

[37] Rashi, commentary on Gen 39:1.

[38] Goldin, "The Youngest Son or Where Does Genesis 38 Belong," 28–29; Coats, "Redactional Unity in Genesis 37–50," 17; and Alter, *The Art of Biblical Narrative*, 6.

[39] Ibn Ezra, commentary on Gen 38:1.

[40] Goldin, "The Youngest Son or Where Does Genesis 38 Belong," 29; Redford, *A Study of the Biblical Story of Joseph*, 18; and Alter, *The Art of Biblical Narrative*, 10.

ii. We should contrast the faithful sexual intercourse of Tamar in B with the faithless activity of Potiphar's wife in C.

Plus a third nexus can be cited.

iii. The fourfold use of *yād(ô)*, '(his) hand,' in 38:28–30 reverberates with the ubiquitous appearance of *yād* in its various forms in 39:1–23.

Ties between A and B and between B and C are important because they bring the Judah and Tamar story into the mainstream of the cycle. But actually all the units of the Joseph Story have catchwords pointing to the next unit, thus further solidifying the redactional unity of these chapters. C and D are linked by the following:

i. *bêt hassōhar*, 'prison-house,' occurs six times in 39:20–23 and twice in 40:3, 40:5.
ii. *śar haṭṭabbāḥîm*, 'chief steward,' appears in 39:1 and 40:3, 40:4.
iii. *sᵉrîs(ê) parᶜōh*, 'officier(s) of Pharaoh,' is used in 39:1 and 40:7.
iv. *bêt ᵓădōnāw*, 'his master's house,' obtains in 39:2 and 40:7.

D and E are both concerned with the famine in Egypt and Canaan and thus share three related catchwords:

i. The word *rāᶜāb*, 'famine,' dominates D and occurs in E in 42:5, 43:1.
ii. The root *šbr*, 'buy grain,' appears frequently in E and is anticipated by D in 41:56–57.
iii. *ᵓōkel*, 'food,' occurs in 41:35 (bis), 41:36, 41:48 (tris) and in 42:7, 42:10, 43:2, 43:4, 43:20, 43:22.

Worked into E and F are the following bridges:

i. Joseph's assistant, *ᵓăšer ᶜal bêtô*, 'he who is over his house,' occurs in 43:16 and 44:1.
ii. The key word *ᵓamtaḥat* and various forms, 'sack,' is used throughout E and F.
iii. *kesep*, 'silver,' appears throughout both units.

iv. Benjamin occupies a central position in E and is the "culprit" in F at 44:12.

v. Juxtaposed at the cusp of the two units are *wayyiškᵉrû*, 'they drank,' in 43:34, and *gᵉbîaᶜ hakkesep*, 'silver goblet,' in 44:2. Though this special possession of Joseph's was used for divining, the appearance of the goblet directly after the drinking scene is probably not coincidental. Indeed it may imply that the brothers should have had a knowledge of Joseph's goblet.

Units F and F′ are not only successive but also correspond within the redactional structuring. Thus the six theme-words shared by F and F′ noted earlier also act as the catchwords linking these pericopes. As the story develops, F′ and E′ are linked by the following nexuses.

i. *wᵉyāšabtā bᵉʾereṣ gōšen*, 'you shall dwell in the land of Goshen,' appears in 45:10; and *yêšᵉbû bᵉʾereṣ gōšen*, 'dwell in the land of Goshen,' occurs in 47:6.

ii. *bānekā ûbᵉnê bānekā*, 'your sons and your grandsons,' is used in 45:10; and *bānāw ûbᵉnê bānāw*, 'his sons and his grandsons,' is used in 46:7.

iii. *ṣōʾnᵉkā ûbᵉqārᵉkā*, 'your flocks and your herds,' obtains in 45:10; and *ṣōʾnām ûbᵉqārām*, 'their flocks and their herds,' occurs in 46:32, 47:1.

iv. *ᶜăgālôt*, 'carts,' is used in 45:19, 45:21, 45:27 and 46:5.

v. *ᶜal ṣawwāʾrāw*, 'upon his neck,' occurs in 45:14 and 46:29 (bis).

vi. The verbal root *klkl*, 'sustain,' is predicated of Joseph in 45:11 and 47:12.

Connecting E′ and D′ are the following links.

i. The word *leḥem*, 'bread,' is used in 47:12 and 47:13.

ii. In E′ Joseph sustains his family and in D′ he provides for all of Egypt.

D′ and C′ have one key catchphrase linking them.

i. In 47:27 we read *wayyēšeb yiśrāʾēl bᵉʾereṣ miṣrayim*, 'Israel dwelled in the land of Egypt'; and in 47:28 we have *wayᵉḥi yaᶜăqōb bᵉʾereṣ miṣrayim*, 'Jacob lived in the land of Egypt.'

C′ and B′ have the following catchwords to bridge the two units.

i. *habbᵉkôr*, 'the firstborn,' occurs in 48:14, 48:18; and *bᵉkôrî*, 'my firstborn,' occurs in 49:3.
ii. *yᵉrēkî*, 'my thigh,' appears in 47:29; and *yarkātô*, 'his flank,' is used in 49:13.
iii. *šᵉkem*, 'Shechem,' in 48:22 reverberates with *šikmô*, 'his shoulder,' in 49:15.

And finally, B′ and A′ are linked with one catchword.

i. The verbal root *ʾsp*, 'gather,' appears in 49:1 and 49:29, 49:33 (bis).

At the outset of this chapter we noted that the Joseph Story is the most unified of the four major cycles in Genesis, and we quoted various authorities to that effect. This conclusion has been borne out thoroughly, highlighted through theme-words shared by matching units and catchwords linking successive units. Standing at the center is the pivot point, the focus of the entire novella, Joseph's disclosure to his brothers. The story begins with only Joseph and his brothers present (A) and ends the same way (A′). It is therefore only fitting that the midway point should include only these very characters. Recognition of the theme-words, catchwords, and pivot point, placed on top of what is already a masterly constructed story filled with emotion and suspense, permits us to reaffirm what earlier readers have already discovered: that the Joseph Story is truly *aḥsana al-qaṣaṣi*, 'the most beautiful of narratives.'[41]

[41] Qurʾān 12:4.

VI

REDACTIONAL STRUCTURING AND SOURCE CRITICISM

The first five chapters of this book demonstrate conclusively that the stories of Genesis are aligned not in an ad hoc or haphazard manner, rather along well-conceived and deliberate lines. In the Primeval History, the compiler established a pattern in 1:1–6:8 which was then repeated (with one necessary alteration) in 6:9–11:26. In the Abraham, Jacob, and Joseph Cycles, sequences were created in 11:27–16:16, 25:19–30:24, and 37:1–44:34 respectively, and then repeated in reverse order in 17:1–22:24, 30:25–35:22, and 45:1–50:26 respectively. The result, when combined with the linking material in 23:1–25:18 and 35:23–36:43, is a redactional structure for all of Genesis. Within this masterful operation we may even note the difference between the ordering of the Primeval History representing pre-Israelite times and that of the Patriarchal Cycles representing Israelite times. In the former the structure is built on purely parallel lines, while in the latter the stories are aligned chiastically. Similarly, the Primeval History stands alone, while the cycles comprising the Patriarchal History are interspersed with the linking material.

Why the final editor of Genesis saw the need for such a redactional structure is difficult to say. His aim may have been theological, that is to say, to show how God's relationship with man and his election of Israel are not haphazard occurrences but are in fact well-established and well-conceived by God himself. Or his goal may have been purely literary, that is, to merely construct a perfectly designed literary unit. As M. Fishbane has noted, similar symmetry and/or chiasm has been detected in Homer's *Iliad*, in the Atraḫasis Epic of ancient Mesopotamia, and in various shorter portions of the Hebrew Bible.[1] Or, more likely, it may have been a combination of both, perhaps with other motivations as well (didactic, mnemonic, etc.). But regardless of the why, we seem to have answered the how. For while we can only speculate as to what the redactor's ultimate aim was, we can uncover how he accomplished his task. In a seminal article on the redaction of Proverbs, Patrick Skehan concluded, "For the first time, it would appear, we know exactly how one Old Testament writer put his book together, and how much he put into it when he did so."[2] Now, it seems, we have a second instance where we have uncovered the modus operandi of an individual who bears ultimate responsibility for the final edition of a biblical book.

The establishment of a basic unity in the Book of Genesis by necessity leads to a discussion of Higher Criticism. The dominant school of Higher Criticism, the Documentary Hypothesis, divides Genesis into three major strands, the Yahwist (J), the Elohist (E), and the Priestly

[1] See the sources cited by M. Fishbane, *Text and Texture* (New York, 1979) 146, nn 4–6; and M. Fishbane, "Composition and Structure in the Jacob Cycle (Gen. 25:19–35:22)," *JJS* 26 (1975) 19, nn 21–26. For a more complete sampling of studies which posit redactional structures in Hebrew and Greek literatures, see J. Dewey, *Markan Public Debate* (Chico, CA, 1980) 34–35, 206–7, nn 125–53. Many thanks to my colleague, Dennis C. Duling, for bringing this reference to my attention. The list of palistrophes complied by A. DiMarco ("Der Chiasmus in der Bibel, 1. Teil," *LB* 36 (1975) 21–97; "Der Chiasmus in der Bibel, 2. Teil," *LB* 37 (1976) 49–68) is impressive but many are either very minor or not present at all.

[2] P. W. Skehan, "Wisdom's House," in *Studies in Israelite Poetry and Wisdom* (Washington, DC, 1971) 45 (revised version of *CBQ* 29 [1967] 162–80).

(P).[3] It is true that recognition of redactional structuring does not a priori militate against the conclusions of the JEDP Theory. Fishbane, for example, in his treatment of the Jacob Cycle, wrote, "This is not to side-step 'documentary' issues. For it is clear that the Jacob Cycle has been composed from numerous traditions. It is, however, the point of this paper to see what was 'done' with these traditions."[4] In other words, it is possible that the Genesis compiler merely took the J, E, and P materials, and edited them in a manner to produce the corresponding sections. This would hold, of course, for the other cycles of Genesis no less than for the Jacob Cycle.

U. Cassuto took a more negative view toward the Documentary Hypothesis in his discussion of redactional structuring in the Abraham Cycle. He concluded, "The perfected form of this structure does not support the view espoused by most modern exegetes, who regard the text as the accidental product of the combination of a number of fragments from various sources. . . . This theory and the problem of the sources of the narratives in general we shall discuss later."[5] Unfortunately, the author's death prevented him from completing this task, though a few pertinent sentences may be culled from the commentary on 12:1–13:5 which survived. But even these statements do not speak to the specific point of how the cycle's unity contradicts the JEDP Theory. Thus it is difficult to predict what route Cassuto would have used.

[3] In this chapter, I speak of the Documentary Hypothesis as a single approach to the Pentateuch. Clearly, I am aware of the faults of this judgment, since not all scholars agree on the various strata and sub-strata, their dates of composition, etc. But it is commonplace, especially in handbooks, textbooks, and introductions to the Bible, to speak of the theory in the singular and to regard it as a scholarly consensus. So without entering into the finesse of the slightly divergent views, I beg the reader's acceptance of the notion that there exists a more or less unified position among biblicists, which would order the sources JEDP and would date them respectively to the 10th, 9th–8th, 7th, and 6th–5th centuries.

[4] Fishbane, "Composition and Structure," 26, n 39.

[5] U. Cassuto, *From Noah to Abraham* (Jerusalem, 1964) 294.

This does not mean that Cassuto's basic assumption is incorrect. Notwithstanding my comments above that redactional unity need not a priori defeat the JEDP Theory, it must be admitted that wherever the basic unity of a section can be established the Documentary Hypothesis can be called into question. This is even more the case when specific evidence can be forwarded to show the failing of this school of source criticism. Let us then proceed to this evidence.

The corresponding units in each of the cycles were seen as parallel not just because of their similar themes and motifs, but just as importantly because of the numerous theme-words which link them. Now, when traditional source criticism assigns corresponding units to different sources, we must wonder how is it that source X uses theme-words a, b, c, d, e, f, g, etc., and that source Y uses the exact theme-words. This is no better seen than in a comparison of 12:1–9 and 22:1–19 (chap. II, units B and B′ [henceforth II.B/B′]). The first of these is usually divided between J (vv 1–4a, 6–9) and P (vv 4b–5) and the second of these is viewed as E. We should ask: how is it that J uses *lek lᵉkā* in 12:1 and that E does so in 22:1; that J uses the second person masculine singular pronoun suffix three times in 12:1 and that E does so in 22:2; that J has Abram go to Moreh in 12:6 and that E takes Abraham to Moriah in 22:2; that J reads *wayyiben šām mizbēaḥ laYHWH* in 12:7 and that E uses *wayyiben šām ʾabrāhām ʾet hammizbēaḥ* in 22:9; that J's blessing in 12:2–3 is remarkably similar to E's blessing in 22:17–18; that J reads *wayyēlek ʾittô lôṭ* in 12:4 and that E states *wayyēlᵉkû šᵉnêhem yaḥdāw* in 22:6, 22:8; that J uses *mᵉqôm* in 12:6 and that E uses *hammāqôm* in 22:3–4, both times meaning 'hallowed site'; that the root *škm* occurs in J in 12:6 and in E in 22:3; that J uses *wayyērāʾ YHWH* in 12:7 and that E includes the toponym *YHWH yirʾeh* in 22:14; that J's story ends in the Negev and that E's story ends in Beersheba; and that both stories have God speaking to the patriarch in two parts, in J at 12:1–3, 12:7, and in E at 22:12, 22:16–18? All of this becomes extremely coincidental and much too difficult to explain if one retains the JEP source analysis of Genesis. The evidence points to one author for these two units.

Similar problems arise in comparing the other matched units. The Creation and Flood units (I.A/A′) are universally divided into J material and P material. But we note the following difficulties: P uses *šbt* in 2:2–3 and J does so in 8:22; J uses *ʿeṣem* in 2:23 and P does so in 7:13; J uses *mithallēk* in 3:8 and P uses *hithallek* in 6:9; J introduces the war instrument *ḥereb* in 3:24 and P does so with *qešet* in 9:13–16; and J uses *derek* in 3:24 and P uses *darkô* in 6:12.

Returning to the Abraham Cycle, we note the similar genealogies (II.A/A′) and note that in each case one important grandchild is singled out, even though 11:27–32 is supposedly P and 22:20–24 is supposedly J. The same holds for those sections which discuss Sarai/Sarah in the foreign palace (II.Ca/C′a). Scholars emphasize the differences in 12:10–20 and 20:1–18 and thus assign the former to J and the latter to E, but the similarities between them as presented in chap. II might also point to just one hand being responsible. We might conclude similarly vis-à-vis the two sections dealing with the parting of one of Abra(ha)m's relatives. 13:5–18 and 21:1–21 (II.Cc/C′c) have plenty of shared theme-words, though once again the respective verses are normally seen as emanating from different sources. Thus, *rîb* in 13:7 is J and *rôbeh* in 21:20 is E; *wayyiśśāʾ lôṭ ʾet ʿênāw wayyarʾ* in 13:10 is J and *wayyipqaḥ ʾĕlôhîm ʾet ʿênehâ wattēreʾ* in 21:19 is E; *miṣrayim* in 13:10 is J and the same word in 21:21 is E; *zarʿăkâ* in 13:15–16 is J and the same word in 21:13 is E; and the root *śym* in 13:16 is J and in 21:18 it is E. Again, it becomes extremely coincidental to assume that J and E have such similar vocabulary when discussing different events, the parting of Abram and Lot and the parting of Abraham and Ishmael.

In the Jacob Cycle the evidence is no less compelling. The initial and final units (III.A/A′) share numerous theme-words and those which appear in verses ascribed to different sources certainly militate against the Documentary Hypothesis. We must wonder how it is that J presents the oracle in 25:23 and that P describes its fulfillment in 35:11–12; that Jacob is named by J in 25:26 and that Israel is introduced by P in 35:10; that the pun on *bkr/brk* occurs in J in 25:31–34 but in P in 35:9–12; and that J uses *rbh* in 25:23 and that P uses this root in 35:11. Using the same two sections but presenting material assigned to J and E now, we can continue to ask how it is that J has Rebekah struggle in childbirth in 25:21–22 and that E has Rachel do likewise in 35:16–20; and that parental differences are highlighted by J in 25:28 and by E in 35:18. If redactional structuring is accepted, it becomes exceedingly difficult for the subscribers to the JEDP Theory to explain these shared theme-words which purportedly emanate from different sources.

As is already apparent, examples such as the above, where the same or similar vocabulary appears in matching units which are usually assigned to different sources, can be multiplied with ease. To show only a few more examples from the Jacob Cycle, we may note *wayyālen šam* in 28:11 from E and in 32:14 from J; *wayyîrāˀ* in 28:17 from E and in 32:8 from J; *maśkurt-* in 29:15 from E and in 31:7, 31:41 from J; *śᵉkārî* in 30:18 from E and in 30:32–33 from J. The first two of these examples are embodied in III.D/D′; the third is in III.E/E′; and the fourth is in III.F/F′. Finally the Joseph Story is no different, with *wayyirˀû* in 37:4 from J and in 50:15 from E; *wayyêlᵉkû* in 37:12 from J and in 50:18 from E; and *ˀbl* in 37:34–35 from E and in 50:10–11 from J; to quote several examples from V.A/A′.[6]

All of this material demonstrates how attention to redactional structuring greatly weakens the Documentary Hypothesis, indeed according to the present writer, renders it untenable. To return to our first example (II.B/B′), it becomes simply incredulous that J wrote 12:1–4a, 12:6–9 about the start of Abraham's spiritual odyssey

[6] On other aspects pertinent to this discussion, see the oft-cited article by R. N. Whybray, "The Joseph Story and Pentateuchal Criticism," *VT* 18 (1968) 522–28.

and that E wrote 22:1–19 about the climax of his spiritual odyssey, and that these two authors living approximately 100 years apart and in different parts of ancient Israel time and again chose the same lexical items. Surely this is too improbable, especially when such examples can be and have been multiplied over and over. Admittedly a corresponding word here or there could be coincidental, but the cumulative nature of the evidence tips the scales heavily against the usual division of Genesis into JEP.

The nexuses which bridge successive units are also problematic for proponents of the Documentary Hypothesis. We will refrain from piling up the evidence as we did for the theme-words, for one good example from the Joseph Story will suffice. We have seen that the Judah and Tamar episode (V.B) is linked to the first unit of this cycle (V.A) with a number of catchwords. 38:1–30 is assigned to J while at least the end of the preceding chapter, 37:29–36 is the work of E. And yet we must ask how it is that E uses *wayᵉšallᵉḥu . . . hakker nāʾ . . . wayyakkîrāh* in 37:32–33 and that J uses *šālᵉḥāh . . . hakker nāʾ . . . wayyakkēr* in 38:25–26; that E uses *nḥm* in 37:35 and that J uses the same root in 38:12; and that E uses *ʿizzîm* in 37:31 and that J does so in 38:17.

The evidence presented here points to the following conclusion: there is much more uniformity and much less fragmentation in the book of Genesis than generally assumed. The standard division of Genesis into J, E, and P strands should be discarded. This method of source criticism is a method of an earlier age, predominantly of the 19th century. If new approaches to the text, such as literary criticism of the type advanced here, deem the Documentary Hypothesis unreasonable and invalid, then source critics will have to rethink earlier conclusions and start anew.

A good place to start might be the Abraham Cycle, for we have seen that the use of Yahweh in 11:27–16:16 and of Yahweh and Elohim in 17:1–22:24 has more to do with the redactional unity of these chapters than with source-critical fragmentation. The use of the name Elohim from 17:3 onward has nothing to do with the proposal that now we have narratives emanating from E and P, rather it marks the pivot point of the Cycle as highlighted also by the patriarch's name change. Higher critics would have a difficult time explaining how J uses Abram in those sections ascribed to him in 11:27–16:16 but Abraham in those sections ascribed to him in 17:1–22:24. The name change in 17:5 supposedly stems from P (presumed by every critic to be post-J); thus how is it that J just happened to use Abram in, for example, the story of Ishmael's birth, but Abraham in, for example, the story of his negotiations with Yahweh to save Sodom and Gomorrah from destruction? These are questions which are not faced by most conventional exegetes; the answers to them bring down the Documentary Hypothesis.

This does not mean that all of Genesis is the work of one author,[7] for there clearly remain different sources and variant traditions. The author of 1:1–2:4a must clearly be someone different than the author of 2:4b–3:24. The tradition which makes Cain a nomad in 4:12–16 is certainly at variance with the one which depicts him building a city in 4:17. But, we must posit one compiler or collator for the Primeval History, one for the Abraham Cycle, one for the Jacob Cycle, and one for the Joseph Story. Whether these four compilers are the same person—in which case we can posit a single editor for the whole book of Genesis[8]—or not, is a question which cannot be answered. But given the systematic working of the entire redactional structure, this would not be a difficult conclusion to reach.[9]

[7] Compare the view of DiMarco, "Der Chiasmus in der Bibel, 1. Teil," 28: "Alle diese wiederholten Chiasmen und Symmetrien [in Gen 1–11] legen nahe, dass es sich um nur einen Autor handelt."

[8] For a parallel see P. W. Skehan, "A Single Editor for the Whole Book of Proverbs," in *Studies in Israelite Poetry and Wisdom*, 15–26 (revised version of *CBQ* 10 [1948] 115–30).

[9] Also pointing to this conclusion are the many excellent points raised by R. L. Cohn, "Narrative Structure and Canonical Perspective in Genesis," *JSOT* 25 (1983) 3–16.

VII

THE DATE OF GENESIS

The major goal of this monograph—to describe the literary technique of the redactor of Genesis—has already been accomplished. But in a work entitled *The Redaction of Genesis*, it seems appropriate to include some information on the date of that redaction, and thus this final chapter. The question, when did Genesis receive its final edited form, has consumed modern biblical scholarship from the outset. The various views are well-known and will not be reviewed here. Moreover, we will progress quite independently, except to refer to the seminal article of Benjamin Mazar, "The Historical Background of the Book of Genesis," in which the Israeli savant proposes the Davidic empire for the period of Genesis' original, and more or less complete, written form.[1] This conclusion, which is by no means Mazar's alone,[2] is accepted here, and evidence to substantiate it will be presented in systematic (though not always detailed[3]) fashion.

The clearest evidence pointing to a Davidic–Solomonic redaction of Genesis are the historical allusions

[1] B. Mazar, "The Historical Background of the Book of Genesis," *JNES* 28 (1969) 73–83.

[2] Even source critics who accept the JEP division would agree to some extent, since the "Yahwistic" material presumably dates from the 10th century.

[3] I realize that much of what I shall say has been pointed out innumerable times, but no attempt is made to cite secondary literature with any consistency or completeness. Also, each point raised could be discussed for pages on end; for economy's sake, however, discussion is kept to a minimum.

present. Clearest of all is 15:18 where the expression "from the river of Egypt to the Great River, the River Euphrates," can only refer to the Davidic boundaries (cf. 1 Kgs 5:1). In the following verses (15:19–21) occur a number of peoples who were not vanquished until David's time. Most important for our present task are the Jebusites, whose city of Jerusalem was captured by David in 2 Sam 5:6–9. The Kenites appear as a distinct ethnic group as late as Saul's time (see 1 Sam 15:6; 27:10). In 1 Sam 30:29 they are associated with David already, after which they disappear from the biblical record. Reference to the Kenizzites cease after Josh 14:14. If they retained any ethnic identity down to the Davidic–Solomonic period, they were certainly subsumed by the empire at that time. The question of the Rephaim is complicated, but we may point out that four individual Rephaim fell to David's forces in 2 Sam 21:15–22. Of Kadmonites, Perizzites, and Girgashites, virtually nothing is known, and exactly who is meant by Hittites, Amorites, and Canaanites is subject to debate, but regardless, subjugation of all these peoples refers clearly to the early monarchy.

The relationship between Jacob and Esau in Genesis is plainly a reflection of Israelite-Edomite affairs during the early monarchy. The oracle to Rebekah that of the two sons "the older shall serve the younger" (25:23), and the blessing of Isaac to Jacob, "you shall be your brothers' master" (27:29), describes Israel's subjugation of Edom under David (2 Sam 8:14). Isaac's words to Esau, "you shall throw off his yoke from your neck" (27:40), refer to the Edomite revolt at the end of Solomon's reign (1 Kgs 11:14–25).

Jacob and Esau are depicted as twins, which is significant in that there appears to have been a closer link between Israel and Edom than, by comparison, between Israel and other nations conquered by David. 2 Sam 8:2 and 8:6 mention tributary exacted from Moab and Aram-Damascus respectively and thus we infer that their kings were allowed to rule as subjects of David. 2 Sam 12:30

states that David merely took the actual crown from the king of Ammon, but it does not imply that the Ammonite king was ousted. In contrast we have reference to the incorporation of Edom as an Israelite province under David (2 Sam 8:14), and of the flight of Edomite royalty to Egypt at the time of the conquest (1 Kgs 11:14–18). The rule of David and Solomon over Edom was firmer,[4] thus Edom was considered more closely linked to Israel, and thus Jacob and Esau are pictured as twins.

The other countries just mentioned also appear in Genesis. Moab and Ammon occur in 19:37–38, where they are genealogically linked to the family of Abraham. This too implies a connection with Israel, and we are to see here a reflection of Davidic–Solomonic rule over the two countries (2 Sam 8:2; 10:6–14). Aram appears throughout the patriarchal stories but the one occurrence which most likely mirrors events of the Davidic period is the agreement between Laban, the Aramean, and Jacob, eponymous ancestor of Israel, at Gilead in 31:45–54. The peaceful resolution of an Aramean-Israelite conflict in the general area of Gilead[5] occurs in 2 Sam 10:19, thus prompting the link between the two episodes.[6]

Returning to Edom for a moment, we naturally should refer to 36:1–43 with its detailed material on Esau's descendants and the Edomite kings. Such a list, most certainly of Edomite origin or at least based on material of Edomite origin, would have been incorporated

[4] Presumably, David and Solomon wished to control the important part of Ezion-geber–Elath and therefore rule over Edom was more direct.

[5] For locating Helam in the general area of Gilead, see H. G. May, ed., *Oxford Bible Atlas* (London, 1962) 65, 127; and Y. Aharoni and M. Avi-Yonah, *The Macmillan Bible Atlas* (New York, 1977) 66–67, 179. Both atlases accept the identification with ᶜAlma.

[6] In this instance, I differ slightly with the view of Mazar ("The Historical Background of the Book of Genesis," 78–79) that the Jacob and Laban pact "is an enlightening portrayal of the relationship between Aram and Israel before the beginning of David's war against the kingdom of Aram-zobah and her allies in Transjordan."

into Israelite literature at a time when Israel had domain over Edom, again during the Davidic–Solomonic empire. Furthermore, 36:31 ("these are the kings who reigned in the land of Edom before a king reigned over the Israelites") suggests that the list originates from the period of the early monarchy. If it were from an earlier period, such a statement would be impossible. If it were from a later period, we would expect an Edomite king list beyond that of the time before 1000, i.e., "before a king reigned over the Israelites."

It may be apposite to quote the theory of A. M. Honeyman[7] who identifies Hadad of 36:39 (as per LXX and 1 Chr 1:51) with the Hadad who revolted against Solomon, Baalhanan of 36:38 with David based on 2 Sam 21:19 where the slayer of Goliath is Elhanan, and Saul of 36:37 with Saul king of Israel (cf. 1 Sam 14:47). There are problems with Honeyman's proposal, e.g., the patronymics of Baalhanan ben Achbor, David ben Jesse, and Elhanan ben Yaare-oregim are all different, and Saul of 36:37 comes from Rehoboth-on-the-River, not Gibeah, but the theory is attractive. If we accept it, we have actual confirmation of 36:31–39 originating in Davidic–Solomonic times. If we do not accept it, we still have the argument of the preceding paragraph which points to the Edomite material's provenance in the period of the United Kingdom.

Another nation common to both the Genesis stories and the Davidic period is the Philistines. I wholeheartedly endorse the theory of Y. M. Grintz and others which holds that the Philistines of the patriarchal narratives are different from the later Philistines of Saul's and David's time.[8] The former is an earlier wave of Aegean emigration, while the latter are among the Sea Peoples who

[7] A. M. Honeyman, "The Evidence for Regnal Names Among the Hebrews," *JBL* 67 (1948) 23–24 and n 44.

[8] Y. M. Grintz, "The Philistines of Gerar and the Philistines of the Coast," in *Studies in Memory of Moses Schorr* (Hebrew; New York, 1945) 96–112; C. H. Gordon, "The Rôle of the Philistines," *Antiquity* 30

reached the Levant in the early 12th century. But the appearance of Philistines in the Abraham and Isaac stories (21:32, 21:34, 26:1, 26:8, 26:14, 26:15, 26:18) and in 1–2 Samuel is not coincidental. The Philistines of the patriarchal narratives may have been used in Davidic times to show that even in Israel's ancient past there were differences between the two peoples. Alternatively, the friendly relationship between Isaac and Abimelech in 26:26–31 may have been used to justify David's peaceful relations with Achish in 1 Sam 27:1–28:2.

We may also see a connection between 14:1–24, especially 14:18–24, and the era of David and Solomon. The identifications of Salem in 14:18 and Jerusalem seems virtually certain.[9] Since the city gained its prominence during the early monarchy, we can see in 14:18–24 an attempt to connect the new capital with Hebrew traditions and with worship of Yahweh already in patriarchal times. By post-Solomonic times it would have been unnecessary to defend the choice of Jerusalem as Yahweh's holy city; the deed would have been a fait accompli. Thus it is harder to argue that 14:18–24 was authored or incorporated into Hebrew literature at a later date. The episode in 14:1–24 also connects Abraham with Damascus (14:15; see also 15:2), perhaps to establish patriarchal links with the city in light of David's occupation of it (2 Sam 8:6).

Other cities associated with the Patriarchs also appear in the stories of David and Solomon. Dan is mentioned in 14:14, and Beersheba in 21:14, 21:31–33, 22:19 (bis), 26:23, 26:33, 28:10, 46:1, 46:5. The two cities form the northern and southern extents of Israel proper during the United Kingdom (2 Sam 24:2, 1 Kgs 5:5). While it is true that the expression "from Dan to Beersheba" occurs as early as Judg 20:1, it ceases to be meaningful after

(1956) 22; U. Cassuto, *From Noah to Abraham* (Jerusalem, 1964) 208; and K. A. Kitchen, *Ancient Orient and Old Testament* (Downers Grove, IL, 1966) 80–81.

[9] E. A. Speiser, *Genesis* (Garden City, NY, 1964) 104; and R. Davidson, *Genesis 12–50* (Cambridge, 1979) 38.

Solomon's death. Instead one finds an expression such as "from Geba to Beersheba" (2 Kgs 23:8) to demarcate the borders of Judah.

Mahanaim occurs in 32:3 and figures prominently in David's career. Abner crowned Ishbosheth king of Israel there in 2 Sam 2:8 and David made it his temporary capital in 2 Sam 17:24, 17:27 during Absalom's revolt. Hebron is obviously of prime importance to the Patriarchs (13:18, 23:2, 23:19, 35:27, 37:14; see also 25:9, 49:30, 50:13) and it is David's first capital in 2 Sam 2:1–4, 5:1–3.[10]

Since so much of the evidence points to the United Kingdom as the time of the redaction of Genesis, we should probably conclude that the patriarchal associations with Bethel antedate Jeroboam I's establishment of the city as a sanctuary site. It is hard to imagine that a later author, presumably a Judean, would have placed Abram at Bethel (12:8, 13:3) and would have made Bethel such an important city in Jacob's life (28:19, 31:13, 35:1–8, 35:15–16). Even those who subscribe to the JEP theory ascribe the first four of these occurrences to J, assumed to be a Judean, and 35:15 is attributed to P, also assumed to be a Judean. Only 35:1–8 and 35:16 are thought to be E, assumed to be an Ephraimite. Moreover, since there is a connection between Samuel and Bethel in 1 Sam 7:16 the Davidic–Solomonic redactor could have had this instance in mind when connecting the Patriarchs with Bethel. The same verse also mentions Mizpah, which we should note appears in 31:49 in the story of Jacob and Laban.

Regardless of the geographical problems involved with 35:19, Rachel's burial spot of Ephrath-Bethlehem is also evoked in stories about David. The two terms occur in 1 Sam 17:12 in connection with Jesse and in Ruth 1:1–2 in connection with David's earlier forebearers. An obvious relationship exists between Ishmael's dwelling

[10] See R. E. Clements, *Abraham and David* (London, 1967) 47–60, for further details, especially regarding the covenant.

"from Havilah by Shur, which is before Egypt," in 25:18, and the exact phrase in 1 Sam 15:7. Finally, the important patriarchal city of Shechem (12:6, 33:18–19, 34:2–26, 35:4, 37:12–14) was, according to Josh 20:7, 21:21, a city of refuge and a Levitical city. Past studies of these cities and the lists in Joshua 20–21 have concluded that they originate in the time of the United Kingdom.[11] In other words, we may tentatively associate even Shechem, although it does not occur in the stories about David and Solomon, with both the Patriarchs and the United Kingdom.

All of this goes to show that there are intimate links between the cities mentioned in the patriarchal narratives and the history of the Davidic–Solomonic period. But we can also expand the geographical discussion somewhat to include tribal material. Two points can be made. First of all we should note that the tribes themselves have an importance in Genesis. The tribal distinctions are emphasized in 29:31–30:24, 35:22–26, 46:8–27, 49:1–27. Such tribal distinctions were most important during the era of the Judges and the early monarchy. From Solomon's time on, however, they decreased in importance. This is not to say that tribal origins were no longer important at all or were no longer known—for even the Mesha Stele refers to Gad, for example—but that 1 Kgs 4:7–19 very clearly introduces a new political alignment to compete with the traditional tribal divisions. In other words, if the tribal system appears so prominently in Genesis, we should see here further evidence for the Davidic–Solomonic period for the book's redaction.[12]

The second point to be raised in this regard is the prominence of Judah in Genesis. Very clearly 38:1–30 is

[11] W. F. Albright, "The List of Levitic Cities," *Louis Ginsberg Jubilee Volume* I (New York, 1945) 49–73; and B. Mazar, "The Cities of the Priests and Levites," *Congress Volume Oxford* (VTSup 7; Leiden, 1960) 193–205.

[12] On the connection between the Israelite tribes and the Davidic period, see N. K. Gottwald, *The Tribes of Yahweh* (Maryknoll, NY, 1979) 358–75.

included to give us an account of David's distant ancestors. We have no similar stories about Jacob's other sons, at least no detailed ones, because our redactor in David's and Solomon's time was mainly interested in the royal lineage which began with Judah and Perez. Judah's prominence is visible in the Joseph Story throughout (37:26, 43:8–9, 44:14–34, 46:28) and of course 49:8–10 is a clear reference to Judah's role as kingly tribe. These references would have been most meaningful to Israelites of the early monarchy, when dynastic succession was evolving as solely a Judahite privilege.

As is well known, Genesis is replete with evidence indicating the antiquity of the book. In the area of tribal associations, we may note that Reuben's position as firstborn, Levi's role as a warrior, and Simeon's geographic tie to Shechem, do not accord with later history and must therefore be ancient traditions. Similarly, the presence of Ishmaelites in 25:12–16, 37:25–28, 39:1, and Midianites in 25:2, 25:4, 36:35, 37:28, 37:36, points to the early origin of the patriarchal traditions. The last historical references to the Ishmaelites are Judg 8:24 (the time of Gideon) and 1 Chr 27:30 (where Obil the Ishmaelite is listed as one of David's officers), with no attestation of the term in a demonstrably post-United Kingdom text.[13] The last historical reference to the Midianites is 1 Kgs 11:18, also of the Davidic–Solomonic period.[14]

There is more evidence which points to the antiquity of Genesis. In regard to onomasticon, we should note that Yahwistic names are wanting in Genesis. They seem to originate with Jochebed in Exod 6:20 and Joshua in

[13] Individual Ishmaelite tribes listed in 25:12–16 appear in later biblical and extra-biblical sources, but this does not affect our conclusion; cf. I. Ephʾal, "Ishmaelites," *EJ* 9 (1971) col. 89; and I. Ephʾal, *The Ancient Arabs* (Jerusalem, 1982) 63.

[14] Cf. Ephʾal, *The Ancient Arabs*, 63. Isa 9:3, 10:26 refer to earlier historical events, and Isa 60:6 uses Midian only in a geographical, not a gentilic, sense. See further O. Eissfeldt, "Protektorat der Midianiter über ihre Nachbarn im letzten Viertel des 2. Jahrtausends v. Chr.," *JBL* 87 (1968) 392–93.

Num 13:16, but remain rare until the early monarchy when names such as Jonathan, Adonijah, Zeruiah, Benaiah, and Jehoiada begin to appear with some regularity. Accordingly, the absence of Yahwistic names in Genesis reflects the antiquity of the traditions. They must antedate the United Kingdom, when they presumably were compiled into their present form more or less. The same holds for the divine names in Genesis. The expressions *paḥad yiṣḥāq* in 31:42, 31:53, *ʾabbir yaʿaqōb* in 49:24, the various *ʾēl* names in 14:18, 16:13, 17:1, 21:33, 28:3, 33:20, 35:11, 43:14, 48:3, and the "God of my/your/his father" concept in 26:24, 28:13, 31:42, 32:10, 46:3, 50:17, are for the most part unique to Genesis. Uniqueness need not a priori be equated with antiquity, but in light of all the data presented, the evidence of divine names may be invoked to argue for the early age of Genesis.

Also well-known are the various customs reflected in Genesis which contradict later Pentateuchal law.[15] Abraham married his half-sister Sarah (20:12) in contrast with the prohibition against such marriages in Lev 18:9, 20:17, Deut 27:22. Jacob married his sister-in-law (28:28) contrary to the law in Lev 18:18. The eclipsing of the firstborn by a younger brother is commonplace in Genesis (17:17–21, 25:29–34, 27:1–40, 38:27–30, 48:13–20, 49:3–4). Even though all the details of Deut 21:15–17 may not apply to each of these episodes, later law makes it clear that the firstborn is not to be denied his birthright and inheritance. Jacob set up a *maṣṣēbâ* (28:18), a practice outlawed in Exod 34:13, Lev 26:1, Deut 12:3, 16:21–22. Abraham planted an *ʾēšel* (21:33), even though Exod 34:13, Deut 12:3, 16:21 prohibit the *ʾăšērâ*, among which Abraham's tamarisk would have to be included. When these laws are to be dated is a difficult and complicated problem. But notwithstanding their usual attribution to D and P and notwithstanding the usual dates ascribed to these two strata, it is also accepted by more and more critics

[15] Much of what follows is indebted to N. M. Sarna, "Genesis, Book of," *EJ* 7 (1971) col. 390.

that much of Pentateuchal law is older than once believed. The legal process was certainly well under way by David's and Solomon's time, so that once again we have evidence for the antiquity of the Genesis stories.

Next we should turn to literary considerations. The Genesis episodes are the epitome of epic literature, and as Cyrus Gordon has pointed out,[16] there are numerous parallels in the epic literatures of other Near Eastern peoples. A major motif of the patriarchal narratives is the quest for an heir through the proper wife. Abraham's relationship with Sarah to produce Isaac is the most detailed version. Isaac's relationship with Rebekah to produce Jacob is told in far fewer verses but it is nonetheless present. And, as noted in chap. III, Jacob's life is not complete until Rachel produces Joseph. This theme is paralleled in the two epics we have from Ugarit, where both Daniel and Kret seek the proper heir. Another theme which permeates Genesis is the Helen of Troy motif. Abraham must twice retrieve Sarah from a foreign palace, Isaac must retrieve Rebekah, and even Dinah needs to be retrieved by her family. This theme occurs in Ugaritic epic, with Kret's rescue of Hurrai, and of course, as its name implies, it is prominent in Greek epic, with Menelaus' retrieval of Helen. The younger child's eclipsing of the firstborn, mentioned above, is paralleled in the Kret Epic with Octavia's superseding her seven brothers. The *nostos*, or homecoming motif, is the main theme of the *Odyssey*, of the Gilgamesh Epic, of various Egyptian tales, and of the Jacob Cycle as well.[17] Even seemingly minor points are paralleled in the other epic literatures. For example, the number 318 in 14:14 is analogous to the number of Hurrian handmaidens plus the bride in an Egyptian scarab of Amenhotep III and to the number dead after four days of fighting in the *Iliad*.[18]

[16] See most importantly, C. H. Gordon, *The Common Background of Greek and Hebrew Civilization* (New York, 1965).

[17] See G. A. Rendsburg, "Notes on Genesis XXXV," *VT* 34 (1984) 361–65.

[18] S. Gevirtz, "Abram's 318," *IEJ* 19 (1969) 110–13.

These and many other parallels which could be cited demonstrate the relative antiquity of the Genesis stories. The Ugaritic, Egyptian, and Babylonian materials are all 2nd millennium traditions. The Greek parallels are harder to date because of the question of the date of Homer. The events described are probably of the 12th century and classicists customarily date Homer to the 9th or 8th century. In other words, Near Eastern epic literature seems to have had its heyday in the 2nd millennium, with the Homeric poems and the Genesis accounts of the early 1st millennium as the culmination and best examples of this literary expression.

What is most interesting is that Hebrew epic[19] tends to disappear from the Bible after the United Kingdom. The Genesis episodes, the Exodus account, the Conquest account, the stories of the Judges, and the rise of David are all told in epic fashion. The material dealing with Solomon acts as a bridge, for there is epic material such as the 480-year figure in 1 Kgs 6:1, though most of his reign is described in very detailed, annalistic fashion. From 1 Kings 12 on, Israelite historiography becomes quite dry, devoid of epic quality.[20] This suggests, consistent with the historical material presented above, that the book of Genesis is not to be dated later than the United Kingdom. From ca. 900 on, due no doubt to the official scribes now

[19] I use this term in the general sense of a long narrative work incorporating historical and presumably ahistorical material, not in the more restricted sense of a lengthy poetic composition of heroic dimension. On this issue, with a focus on a possible epic *Vorlage* to the present Pentateuchal narrative, see the admirable essay by C. Conroy, "Hebrew Epic: Historical Notes and Critical Perspectives," *Biblica* 61 (1980) 1–30. I disagree with Conroy's conclusion (pp. 29–30) that the terminological question has substantive implications. Thus, I see no harm in continuing to refer to early Israelite literature as "Hebrew epic," by which one can intend prose and/or poetry. It hardly needs to be added that this usage is quite common in biblical studies; indeed this precipitated Conroy's study.

[20] A notable exception are the stories about Elijah and Elisha, suggesting perhaps that epic writing continued in northern Israel longer than in southern Judah.

active in Jerusalem, historical writing is annalistic. In the period before the establishment of a bureaucracy, epic narrative of the type found in Genesis was the norm. One sure piece of evidence in this regard, *Frauengeschichten*, the spice of epic, are prominent up to David's time, somewhat present in Solomon's reign, and virtually absent from Rehoboam on.

Finally, we may garner some linguistic evidence in favor of a 10th century date for the redaction of Genesis. In a recent article,[21] I have argued that the 3rd person common singular pronoun *hwʾ* in Genesis (and throughout the Pentateuch) suggests an earlier Hebrew layer than that which uses *hwʾ* for the masculine and *hyʾ* for the feminine in Joshua through Chronicles. The move from epicene *hwʾ* to gender-distinguished *hwʾ/hyʾ* probably has the internationalism and the expanded boundaries of the United Kingdom as its catalyst, especially since it can be demonstrated that other Canaanite dialects and indeed all of Semitic distinguish gender for the 3rd person singular pronoun.

Another linguistic item which can be forwarded is the presence of three dual pronominal suffixes in Genesis, at 18:20, 19:9 (both third person forms) and 31:9 (second person form). In two other studies,[22] I have demonstrated that, although such forms do appear sporadically in late works, a bunching of them suggests an early date of composition. No specific cut-off date was offered, but it is noteworthy that in prose narrative, the last such forms occur in 1 Sam 6:7 (tris), 6:10 (bis), 6:12, and Ruth 1:8, 1:9, 1:11, 1:13, 1:19, 4:11. In other words, in no demonstrably post-Solomonic historical text (e.g., 1 Kings 12–2 Kings 25, all of Chronicles, Ezra, Nehemiah, Esther) do such forms occur.

21 G. A. Rendsburg, "A New Look at Hebrew *HWʾ*," *Biblica* 63 (1982) 351–69.

22 G. A. Rendsburg, "Late Biblical Hebrew and the Date of 'P,'" *JANESCU* 12 (1980) 77; and G. A. Rendsburg, "Dual Personal Pronouns and Dual Verbs in Hebrew," *JQR* 73 (1982) 38–58.

Also of a linguistic nature are the Egyptian names in the Joseph Story. Various studies have dated the names, or better the name types, to various periods, from as early as the 19th Dynasty, the time of Moses,[23] to as late as Saite and Persian times.[24] Neither of these extremes is correct, however. A more sober study of the names by A. R. Schulman concludes that "the Egyptian names, all of which are of approximately the same date, argue for the writing of the stories to be dated to a time when these names were in current usage, to the time of the late Twenty-first to Twenty-second Dynasties, which corresponds in historical biblical chronology to the period of David and Solomon."[25] A thorough knowledge of Egypt, which the author of the Joseph Story very clearly possessed, would have been accessible at this time given the contact between Israel and Egypt during the 900s.[26]

The mass of evidence very clearly supports a redaction for the Book of Genesis during the United Kingdom. The historical allusions adduced mainly by Mazar, various indications of the book's antiquity, the literary style, and the linguistic data all merge in the Davidic–Solomonic era. During this period we can assume that literary activity reached new heights in ancient Israel.[27] The authorship/compilation/redaction of Genesis was but one of the literary achievements of this era. Concurrently, much more of the biblical historical material was being composed, especially the Davidic Court History (2 Samuel 9–20, 1 Kings 1–2) and no doubt other portions of our canonical books of Samuel. In this manner we are able to explain the

[23] J. Vergote, *Joseph in Égypte* (Louvain, 1959) 141–50.

[24] D. B. Redford, *A Study of the Biblical Story of Joseph* (Leiden, 1970) 228–31.

[25] A. R. Schulman, "On the Egyptian Name of Joseph: A New Approach," *SAK* 2 (1974) 235–43, especially 243.

[26] See A. Malamat, "Aspects of the Foreign Policies of David and Solomon," *JNES* 22 (1963) 1–17.

[27] See J. Bright, *A History of Israel* (2nd ed.; Philadelphia, 1972) 214–15; and C. H. Gordon, *The Ancient Near East* (New York, 1965) 166–67.

many similar expressions in Genesis and 2 Samuel 11–15 collated by Benno Jacob,[28] the historical connections discussed earlier, and perhaps even U. Cassuto's tentative proposal that 20:1–18 parallels the Philistine capture and return of the ark in 1 Samuel 4–6.[29] This chapter on the date of the redaction has been by necessity extremely economical. Further research, it is hoped, will garner even more evidence and point out still other similarities, literary, historical, and otherwise, between Genesis and the United Kingdom.[30]

[28] B. Jacob, *Genesis: Das erste Buch der Tora* (Berlin, 1934) 1048–49.

[29] U. Cassuto, *From Noah to Abraham* (Jerusalem, 1964) 341.

[30] See, e.g., R. Alter, *The Art of Biblical Narrative* (New York, 1981) 117, 120, for connections between 1 Samuel 18 and Genesis 39 and between 1 Samuel 19 and Genesis 31. See also, though I do not agree with all his conclusions, W. Brueggemann, "David and His Theologian," *CBQ* 30 (1968) 156–81.

INDEX

Genesis

1:1	13
1:2	9
1:4	23
1:9	9
1:21	10
1:22	9
1:25	10
1:27	10
1:28	9, 10, 11
1:29	11
2:1–2	11
2:2–3	10, 11, 103
2:4	13
2:4a	23
2:4b	23
2:5	11
2:7	11
2:7–8	11
2:10–14	16
2:21	11
2:23	11, 103
2:25	23
3:1	23
3:8	11, 103
3:24	11, 12, 23, 103
4:1–2	14
4:3	14
4:3–5	14
4:4–5	14
4:7	14
4:8	14, 15
4:10	14
4:11	14
4:12	14
4:12–16	106
4:14	15, 24
4:15	24
4:16	16
4:17	16, 17, 106
4:19	17
4:21	17
4:22	17
4:24	18, 24
4:25	17
4:26	16, 17, 24
5:1–2	19
5:1–3	112
5:2	24
6:1	20, 21, 24
6:1–4	21
6:2	20
6:4	20
6:5	21, 23
6:5–8	21, 22
6:6–7	21
6:6–8	21
6:7	20
6:8	22, 23, 24
6:8–9	23, 25
6:9	11, 22, 23, 24, 103
6:12	12, 103
6:16	11
6:17–18	12
6:19	10
6:19–21	12
6:20	10
6:22	12
7:1–3	12
7:3	10
7:4	11, 12
7:5	12
7:6–12	12
7:9	10
7:10	11

Genesis (cont.)

7:11 9
7:13 11, 103
7:13–24 12
7:14 10
7:15–16 11
7:16 10, 11
7:22 11
8:1 9
8:1–12 12
8:2 9
8:10 11
8:12 11
8:13 9
8:13–14 12
8:17 9
8:21 11
8:22 10, 103
9:1 9, 10, 11, 24
9:2 10
9:3 11
9:6 10
9:13–16 11, 103
9:18 14, 24
9:19 14
9:20 14
9:21 14
9:22 14, 15
9:23 15
9:24 14
9:25 14
9:29 24
10:1 24
10:2 16
10:5 24
10:6 16
10:6–8 18
10:7 18
10:8–12 16
10:9 16
10:10 16
10:11 16, 18
10:20 24
10:21 16, 17
10:22 18
10:28 18
10:29 18
10:31 24
11:1 20, 21, 24
11:3 20
11:4 20, 21, 24
11:5 20, 21
11:6 20, 21, 23
11:7–9 21
11:8 20
11:9 20
11:10 19, 24
11:26 23, 27, 51
11:27 27, 29
11:28 47
11:29 30
11:30 30
11:31 47
11:32 51
12:1 31, 47, 102
12:1–3 33, 102
12:2 32
12:2–3 34, 102
12:3 32
12:4 32, 102
12:5 32, 47
12:6 31, 32, 33, 47, 102, 113
12:7 31, 33, 47, 102
12:8 47, 48, 112
12:9 48
12:11 35
12:12 36
12:13 36
12:14–15 36
12:15 36
12:16 36
12:17 36
12:18 36
12:19 36
13:1 36, 48
13:2 37, 48
13:3 48, 112
13:4 37, 48
13:4–7 38
13:7 37, 47, 103
13:10 37, 48, 103
13:11 47
13:12 48
13:14–17 37
13:15 47
13:15–16 37, 103
13:16 37, 103
13:18 48, 112
14:2 39, 40, 48
14:3 40
14:5 48

14:7	48
14:8	40, 48
14:10	40
14:12	48
14:13	40, 48
14:14	48, 111, 116
14:15	48, 111
14:16	40
14:18	40, 48, 111, 115
14:18–24	111
14:19	40, 41
14:20	40, 46, 48
14:21	48
14:22	40, 41, 46
15:1	41, 42, 48
15:2	48, 111
15:3	42
15:4–5	42
15:6	43, 44, 48
15:7	42, 43, 44
15:9–11	42
15:9–12	44
15:10	48
15:13	42
15:13–16	42, 44
15:14	48
15:16	48
15:17	42, 44
15:18	48, 108
15:19–21	108
15:20	48
15:21	48
16:1–6	44
16:7–14	38
16:7–16	44
16:10	49
16:11	44, 49
16:11–16	49
16:13	46, 115
16:13–14	44
16:15–16	38, 45
16:16	49
17:1	41, 42, 49, 51, 52, 115
17:1–5	46, 52
17:2	42, 49
17:3	106
17:4	42
17:5	106
17:6	42, 55
17:7–8	44
17:8	42, 55
17:8–10	38
17:10–14	42, 44
17:15	42
17:15–22	42, 44
17:17–21	115
17:20	49
17:23–27	42, 44
17:27	112
18:1	40, 49, 51
18:1–8	44
18:2	49
18:3–8	49
18:9–15	38
18:9–16	44
18:10	44
18:12–15	49
18:18	40, 49
18:19	40
18:20	118
18:20–21	49
18:23	39
18:23–28	40
18:25	39
18:26	49
18:32	40
18:33	40
19:1	49
19:2–3	49
19:3	40
19:4	40
19:6	49
19:7	39
19:9	39, 118
19:15	49
19:16	49
19:17	40
19:19	39, 40
19:19–20	40
19:20	40
19:22	40
19:23	41
19:23–24	40, 41
19:24	40, 41
19:26	40
19:32–35	49
19:36	49
19:37–38	109
20:1–18	120
20:2	35, 36
20:3	36
20:3–4	36

Genesis (cont.)

20:6 36
20:7 36
20:9 36
20:11 36
20:12 115
20:14 36
20:17–18 39
20:18 36
21:1–2 39
21:1–3 38
21:1–7 37, 38, 45
21:2 49
21:13 37, 103
21:14 111
21:18 37, 49, 103
21:19 37, 49, 103
21:20 37, 103
21:21 37, 103
21:27 37, 49
21:31 36
21:31–33 111
21:32 111
21:33 37, 46, 49, 115
21:34 111
22:1 50, 102
22:2 31, 102
22:3 32, 102
22:3–4 32, 33, 102
22:6 32, 49, 102
22:8 32, 102
22:9 31, 102
22:12 33, 102
22:14 33, 102
22:15 34
22:15–18 33
22:16–18 33, 102
22:17 32
22:17–18 34, 102
22:18 32
22:19 49, 111
22:20 50
22:21 30
22:23 29
23:2 112
23:19 112
24:3 74
24:37 74
25:2 114
25:4 74, 114
25:6 74
25:7 75
25:8 75
25:9 75, 112
25:12–16 114
25:13 76
25:18 113
25:19 1, 68
25:20 55
25:21–22 55, 104
25:21–23 38
25:21–26 56
25:23 54, 55, 104, 108
25:24–26 38
25:26 55, 104
25:27 55, 56
25:28 55, 73, 104
25:29–34 55, 115
25:31–34 55, 104
25:33 67
26:1 111
26:4 58
26:7 57, 58
26:8 111
26:9 58
26:10 58
26:14 58, 111
26:15 111
26:18 111
26:22 58
26:23 111
26:24 115
26:26 58
26:26–31 111
26:26–33 58
26:28 58
26:29 58
26:31 58
26:32–34 67
26:33 111
26:34–35 67, 68
27:1–40 115
27:10 59
27:13 73
27:14 59
27:16 60
27:18–29 59
27:21–22 60
27:23 60
27:25–27 60
27:26–27 59

27:27–29 67
27:28 60
27:29 60, 108
27:36 60
27:38 60
27:40 60, 108
27:41–45 59
27:46–28:9 67
28:2–7 60
28:3 115
28:5 59
28:6–7 60
28:10 62, 68, 111
28:11 62, 104
28:11–19 62
28:12 62
28:13 62, 63, 115
28:13–15 63, 67
28:14 62
28:15 63
28:17 63, 104
28:18 63, 67, 115
28:19 63, 112
28:22 63
28:28 115
29:1 74
29:1–10 64
29:3 64
29:4 64
29:8 64
29:10 64, 67
29:11 64
29:13 64
29:14 64
29:15 64, 104
29:20–30 64
29:22 64
29:23–26 64
29:23–30 67
29:25 64
29:25–26 72
29:31–35 53
29:31–30:24 113
29:32–30:23 65
30:14–16 65
30:18 65, 104
30:22–24 66, 67, 81
30:22–25 66, 69
30:25 66, 67
30:28 65
30:32–33 65, 104
30:32–43 67
30:35–37 65
30:37–43 65
30:39 65
31:4–12 64
31:7 64, 104
31:8–12 67
31:9 118
31:13 112
31:20 64
31:26 64
31:28 64, 67
31:32 64
31:33–35 64
31:38–39 64
31:41 64, 104
31:42 115
31:44 64
31:45–54 109
31:46 64
31:49 112
31:53 115
31:54 64
32:1 62, 63, 67
32:2 62
32:3 63, 68, 112
32:4 62
32:4–22 67
32:7 62
32:8 63, 104
32:10 63, 115
32:10–13 63
32:13 63
32:14 62, 104
32:27 62
32:29 55
32:30 62
32:31 62, 63
32:33 55, 63, 68
33:1–2 59
33:1–8 59
33:3 60
33:4 59, 60
33:5–7 60
33:5–11 67
33:6–7 60
33:9 60
33:11 59
33:14 60
33:16 60
33:17 61

Genesis (cont.)

33:18	59, 60, 61
33:18–19	113
33:19	67, 68
33:20	55, 115
34:1–27	67
34:2	58
34:2–26	113
34:5	58
34:7	58
34:7–31	67
34:8–23	58
34:9	58
34:10	58
34:11	58
34:12	58
34:13	58
34:13–29	57
34:14	57, 58
34:21	58
34:22	58
34:23	58
34:25–26	58
35:1	55
35:1–7	56
35:1–8	112
35:4	113
35:5	67
35:7	55
35:8	56
35:9	55
35:9–12	55, 104
35:9–15	56
35:10	55, 104
35:11	55, 104, 115
35:11–12	54, 104
35:15	112
35:15–16	112
35:16	112
35:16–20	55, 56, 104
35:18	55, 104
35:19	112
35:21	55, 56
35:21–22	55, 56
35:22	55, 68
35:22–26	113
35:26	74
35:27	75, 112
35:28	75
35:29	75
36:2	74
36:10	76
36:31	110
36:31–39	110
36:35	114
36:37	110
36:38	110
36:39	110
36:43	68
37:1	81
37:2	1, 81
37:4	81, 104
37:7	81
37:9	81
37:10	81
37:12	81, 82, 104
37:12–14	113
37:14	112
37:15–17	82
37:18	82
37:20	81
37:25–28	114
37:26	114
37:28	114
37:31	94, 105
37:32	81, 93
37:32–33	82, 93, 105
37:33	81
37:34–35	82, 104
37:35	94, 105
37:36	114
38:1	86, 94
38:3	84
38:4	84, 85
38:5	84
38:6	84, 85
38:7	84
38:8	84, 85
38:9	84, 85
38:11	84
38:12	94, 105
38:12–13	85
38:14	84, 85
38:15	85
38:15–19	84
38:16	86
38:17	85, 86, 94, 105
38:18	84, 85
38:19	85
38:20	85, 86
38:23	86

38:24	86	44:3	91
38:25	84, 93	44:8	91
38:25–26	93, 105	44:11	91
38:26	84	44:12	91, 96
38:27–30	115	44:14–34	114
38:28–30	95	44:18–34	91
39:1	94, 95, 114	44:28	92
39:2	95	45:1–4	92
39:4	87	45:5	92
39:5	87	45:9	91
39:6	87, 88	45:10	96
39:7–14	87	45:11	96
39:8	87	45:12	91
39:9	87	45:13	91
39:20–23	95	45:14	91, 96
39:21	87	45:19	96
40:3	95	45:21	91, 96
40:4	95	45:22	91
40:5	95	45:27	96
40:7	95	46:1	111
40:19	89	46:3	90, 115
40:22	89	46:5	90, 96, 111
41:5	89	46:6	91
41:22	89	46:6–27	90
41:34	89	46:7	96
41:35	95	46:8	91
41:36	95	46:8–27	113
41:48	89, 95	46:27	91
41:54–55	89	46:28	90, 91, 114
41:56–57	89, 95	46:29	96
42:1–2	90	46:30	90
42:5	95	46:32	96
42:7	95	46:34	90
42:10	90, 95	47:1	96
42:11	90	47:3	90
42:13	90	47:4	90
43:1	95	47:6	96
43:2	95	47:12	96
43:3–10	90	47:13	89, 96
43:4	95	47:14	89
43:4–5	90	47:19	89
43:5	90	47:20	89
43:7	90	47:21	89
43:8–9	114	47:22	89
43:14	115	47:23	89
43:16	95	47:24	89
43:20	95	47:26	89
43:22	95	47:27	96
43:34	96	47:28	96
44:1	91, 95	47:29	87, 97
44:2	91, 96	47:30	87

Genesis (cont.)

47:31 87
48:3 87, 115
48:7 87, 88
48:9 87
48:13–20 115
48:14 87, 97
48:15 87
48:16 87
48:17 87
48:18 97
48:19 87
48:20 87
48:21–22 83
48:22 97
49:1 97
49:1–27 113
49:3 85, 97
49:3–4 115
49:7 85
49:8–10 114
49:8–12 84
49:10 84, 85
49:11 84, 85
49:13 97
49:15 86, 97
49:17 86
49:19 86
49:24 115
49:28 81
49:29 81, 83, 97
49:30 112
49:31 72
49:33 97
50:4 81
50:5 82
50:10–11 82, 104
50:11 82
50:13 81, 112
50:15 81, 104
50:17 81, 115
50:18 82, 104
50:20 81
50:21 81, 82

Exodus

2:6 81
2:20 88
6:3 46
6:20 114
34:13 115

Leviticus

18:9 115
18:18 115
20:17 115
26:1 115

Numbers

13:16 115

Deuteronomy

12:3 115
16:21 115
16:21–22 115
21:15–17 115
27:22 115

Joshua

14:14 108
20:7 113
21:21 113

Judges

8:24 114
14:1 85
20:1 111

1 Samuel

4–6 120
6:7 118
6:10 118
6:12 118
7:16 112
14:47 110
15:6 108
15:7 113
17:12 112
18 120
19 120
27:1–28:2 111
27:10 108
30:29 108

2 Samuel

2:1–4 112
2:8 112
5:6–9 108
8:2 108, 109
8:6 108, 111
8:14 108, 109
10:6–14 109
10:19 109
11–15 120
12:30 108
17:24 112
21:15–22 108
21:19 110
24:2 111

1 Kings

4:7–19 113
5:1 108
5:5 111
6:1 117
11:14–18 109
11:14–25 108
11:18 114

2 Kings

23:8 112

Isaiah

9:3 114
10:26 114

Jonah

3:1 34

Psalms

116:8–9 42

Ruth

1:1–2 112
1:8 118
1:9 118
1:11 118
1:13 118
1:19 118
4:11 118

1 Chronicles

1:51 110
27:30 114